A GIFT FRO

A GIFT FROM SEBASTIAN

BⵊXTREE

To my beloved father, whose troubled faith was shattered by Supi's death, that he may be delighted to find out he was wrong – that there is a Disneyland up there – and that he and his grandson are together on the rides.

First published in hardback in Great Britain in 1995 by Boxtree Limited, Broadwall House, 21 Broadwall, London SE1 9PL

This paperback edition published in Great Britain in 1996 by Boxtree Limited

1 3 5 7 9 10 8 6 4 2

ISBN 0 7522 0597 8

Cover designed by Shoot That Tiger!
Typeset by SX Composing, Rayleigh, Essex
Printed and bound in Great Britain by
Cox and Wyman Ltd, Reading

A CIP catalogue entry for this book is available from the British Library

Introduction

Dr Stanley Rom picked our little baby up in his hands, and looked him straight in the eyes. Our little boy, who at just two weeks old had already fought so hard to live. Now he was well enough to come home to meet his brothers – and truly become a part of the family. His eyes shone with the milky innocence of brand new babyhood as he nestled in those hands, those huge physician's hands which had delicately and intricately performed the tasks necessary to save his life, and which now cradled him completely within their span.

Mike and I looked on in awe and relief that the tense weeks of special care had ended, and he was now ours again, to love and nurture without tubes, drips and monitors. I longed to take off his hospital robe and dress him in our baby sleepsuit, and wrap him in the same shawl which had warmed our other sons.

'Your baby is quite well,' said Dr Rom, with an affectionate smile. Then he turned back to Sebastian and lifted him closer to his face. 'Now, young man, you go out and make your mark in the world!'

Tears welled up in my eyes. I was already so proud of my little boy. How could I possibly have known then what would happen to Sebastian, and quite how he would make his mark?

Like all babies, he seemed to radiate love and light. He was a beautiful child. But then I would think that – I am his mum. He was wise, diplomatic, clever and loving. And above all, Sebastian knew something the rest of us didn't know. I cannot describe it better than that, because I do not understand it.

A friend of a friend of mine lost his ten-year-old daughter in

1

a road accident. He said she had always been a different sort of child from others. He had always thought, long before she died, that she had 'a mature spirit'. She had been a loving, laughing, spontaneous little girl like all others, but there was always something else – an unfathomable maturity. I understand now what he meant – because Sebastian had that, too. My family know that I'm not just clouding my memory with sentimentality. We all felt it. A maturity of spirit.

It was a chance remark – but I caught my mother-in-law saying it to Mike in the kitchen one day. She'd just finished giving Sebastian his bottle, and had been staring deep into his eyes and cooing at him, enjoying the special closeness you get when you're feeding a much loved baby. She wouldn't have said it if she'd known I was near. But I'd been upstairs fetching something, and was returning down the steps to the basement area. She was talking about Sebastian.

'I don't know why I feel it, but he's only on loan to us, this one,' she said. And Mike agreed.

Silently, so did I. Or rather, I knew what they meant – though I wouldn't have dared articulate it. Our children are only ever 'on loan' to us. We are there to love, teach and guard them for as long as we can – but one day, we know they will fly. Sebastian somehow knew it, too.

A wonderful letter arrived at my door one day, from a lady in Eastbourne, a Mrs Rylands, who tried to explain that Sebastian would indeed have known his destiny. 'We all have to work out our own "karma", and put right whatever we may have missed in a previous life,' she wrote.

She said Sebastian would have sat down with God, and worked out his final task on earth, before reaching Heaven. 'Sebastian already knew he would only be with you for a short while. God chose him especially for a purpose – but because he was an experienced and fulfilled soul, it was not necessary for him to spend very long here.'

'If I had lost a baby in the same way it wouldn't have got the same publicity,' she said in her letter. But, she said, Sebastian chose his parents, the time and the place wisely, in order to get something done. Of course you'll grieve, she said. But also remember that through you, Sebastian has achieved his karma.

I like that.

Of course, you probably know now what did happen to him. Four months after we celebrated his homecoming from maternity hospital, and on the morning of his brother's birthday, I found Sebastian dead in his cot. The pain of losing him is still like a constant living laceration in my body. And my heart will never accept it.

I have my wonderful photographs, though, and they help me through the worst days. But so many of my shots of Sebastian are of him lying down, on his tummy, fast asleep. The only moments when I had enough time, and hands free, to pick up a camera were, ironically, when he was sleeping. On his tummy, always on his tummy. It stabs at me now, like a fresh wound every time, the sight of him sleeping so cosily on his tummy, arms up, his perfect little fingers almost caressing his nose, his eyes tight shut but edged with long black lashes.

If only I had known, my dear little Supi. I would have turned you over. If only I had known.

Chapter 1: July 1990

It was a picture-postcard start to a perfect holiday – the sun was hot, the sea blue, the hotel was perfect and there was a cosy little spot by the baby pool which we adopted as our own. Like cats coming in from the cold, we slowly unfurled in the heat, watching the children run, jump and splash in a frenzy of new-found freedom. Mike ordered Brandy Sours, the traditional cocktail of the island. I leaned back and closed my eyes, knowing I could trust our nanny, Alex, to keep hers on the blur of fluorescent armbands and floppy sunhats which was our kids. This was real relaxation. Heaven. This was Cyprus as we knew it.

At lunchtime the parasols went up, and an olive-skinned waiter in cool, crisp cotton brought the customary poolside snack of Greek meze and Village Salad – with the ever-present Coke. Mike and I escaped upstairs to the silence and seclusion of our suite, looked down on the pool scene below, and thought how lucky we were, and how happy. Here, in cool, air-conditioned luxury, stark contrast to the human barbecue below, you could feel your skin tingle with goose-bumps.

Mike drew the curtains, and in the gentle shade, we made love. We made Sebastian.

I know the exact day only because we had joked about it at the time. The night before, Cyprus Airways had lost one of our bags. It had gone to Athens, or stayed in London, or done the round trip – we never found out quite where it had gone, why it had been separated from the others, nor why it took two days to trace and recover.

It was one of those flights which sounds sensible when you

5

book it, but lands you at the inhuman hour of one in the morning on a foreign piece of tarmac, arguing with Jobsworth airport officials who don't speak your language. All suitcases had been unceremoniously dumped on the runway, because the baggage handler had gone home to sleep. So there was a mad scramble while the stalwart passengers found their own luggage, and dragged each piece to the customs hut. Mike's was the one case missing. Another passenger said he thought a young boy had taken it. By the time we found that a young schoolboy had already passed through customs and been collected by his Army parents and taken off home to the British military base, an hour had gone by.

Cypriot tempers were rising. The Jobsworth officials couldn't understand why Mike was so unimpressed, and was using words their dictionaries did not explain. When I saw the clock reach 3 am I had had enough. Alex was almost asleep, holding our toddler, Jamie – who appeared comatose and was dribbling down her blouse. Oliver, just three years old, was sitting astride his suitcase, moaning in dismay. The novelty of staying up late had long expired. Mike and a man in a peaked cap were embroiled in a heated exchange about whether or not you could be forcibly deported from a country if you hadn't actually got as far as immigration.

There's only one thing for it, I thought, slightly ashamed of my decision. I would have to play the little woman. I would have to cry. I started to sob loudly, clutching Oliver for dramatic support. He immediately augmented my image of despair.

It worked. They all apologized, and I was offered several grubby handkerchiefs. Mike withdrew his flowery insult, made several hours earlier to a stewardess who'd long since gone to her bed, and the whole ugly matter was forgotten. We managed to find our extremely patient, and by now very rich, taxi driver outside the airport arrivals gate, and we were off. On our hols at last. Thankfully intact, except for one bag.

But it had been Mike's suitcase – with the all-important toiletries. And I wasn't on the pill. So we should have known the risks of making love that day. 'It'll be Cyprus Airways' fault!' we quipped, never thinking for a second that another baby could possibly be on his way. Not just like that.

It was the happiest holiday I have ever had – and I delight now in thinking that the little cluster of cells which became Sebastian's life was busily dividing and subdividing inside me while I was so content. And, of course, blissfully unaware that I was pregnant. Because the reality hit me weeks later like a sledgehammer. The time simply wasn't right to be enlarging the family again. Too much was going on. Life had suddenly become very complicated and job security was at an all-time low. Things were going wrong at work – in fact they had been going awry almost since I had transferred from the daily routine of presenting *Good Morning Britain* to the Sunday current affairs slot.

It hadn't been my idea – it was the opportunist brainwave of TV-am's managing director, Bruce Gyngell. He had rung me in Australia, where I was spending maternity leave following the birth of son number two, Jamie, to suggest I think of retiring from the high-profile daily show to Sundays. Until then, David Frost had occupied the slot, filling it with politicians and other headline makers. He never failed to get an interview with a prime minister or two when he wanted but, somehow, I felt – along with other production staff at TV-am – that the programme lacked friendliness and warmth. So, I was excited when Bruce told me that David was leaving TV-am to host a new current affairs show in America. I was thrilled – for David, and for myself.

Bruce seemed almost angry that Frost had left him, but was pleased he had found a solution which would mean hanging on to me. He had been conscious that I might want to leave, now that I had two young children. 'Now I'm left with a load of Sunday shows and no-one to present them. I think it's a great time for you to move in.... What do you think ? You can't go on getting up at three every morning with two young children.'

He was dead right. This was the perfect answer to my problem – the ideal job for a working media mum. I said yes almost before Bruce had asked the question.

'Right,' he bellowed, deal done. 'We'll fax a contract out to you – and my advice is to sign fast in case David's show flops and he comes back for his old job.'

We laughed – but I didn't realize then that his words were based on a real fear and that just a few weeks later, and before I was due to receive that fax, David Frost would be returning.

For some strange reason, that fax never reached me. Whenever I rang TV-am to ask why, the only answer I ever got was 'lawyers'. Bruce couldn't figure it out either. Things weren't progressing as he had wanted. And all the time stories were abounding in the press about Frosty's 'flop' programme in New York. Already, the rumour machine at work was speculating that he would soon return and want his Sunday shows back. Eventually, Bruce came out to Australia himself, on holiday. I was summoned to meet with him at Kerry Packer's sunshine home on Palm Beach, north of Sydney.

The Packers' tame kookaburra was being fed scraps of meat, perched on the wooden balcony, as I walked into the family living-room and was greeted with a hearty slap on the back from Kerry and a tearful hug from Bruce. Emotion always played openly on Bruce's face – and he was genuinely happy to see me. I think he'd always had a soft spot for me and always will.

They ushered me over to a quiet spot on the gigantic verandah, which had breathtaking views of the bay, the sand and the surf, now and then eclipsed by swaying eucalyptus trees. Bruce took a pen out of his shirt pocket – as ever in pale pink and embroidered B.G. – and scribbled a list of dates on a sheet of white paper.

'We still don't know about Frost,' he said in a quick,

businesslike manner, 'but for the moment we want you to present Sundays from the week you get back, through to the summer. Then we'll leave thirteen weeks free during the summer for...er...other projects – I might want to try out some new talent – and then you'll come back on in the autumn through to Christmas. As for 1990 – we'll have to see about dates later. Because David might well be back by then. But you can take it from me that you'll have at least half the year – we may just have to sort out dates between you and David.'

It sounded great news to me. So what about a formal contract? I had learned long ago that nothing counts in TV unless it's written, preferably in blood.

'We'll have that ready for you to sign as soon as you get back. I promise,' said Bruce. And he and Kerry sealed it with a drink, a long cocktail on ice, dreamed up by the bronzed, half-naked male housekeeper who was flitting about in the open-plan kitchen. This is the life, I thought. But I had to decline the offer of lunch because husband, children, in-laws and my mother and sister, who had all joined us on our three-month Australian holiday, were waiting on the beach below.

Mike and Bruce had been sworn enemies since the days of Mike's sacking from TV-am, so I thought I ought to make a hasty exit lest the two men should meet. I needn't have worried. Bruce spotted Mike strolling along the sand and walked up to him, arms outstretched. There was sincere delight on the part of both men to talk again. But they carefully avoided professional banter. Instead, the talk was of Australia and how we didn't really want to go home.

Bruce later became the boss of Channel Nine in Sydney, and more recently the Chief Executive of Yorkshire Tyne Tees Television back in Britain. How I'd love to work for him again. There never was a more colourful boss, nor a less predictable. His moods could change faster than the wind. But if he loved you, deep down, he would never forget.

The show was called *Diamond on Sunday*, the title sequence

featuring scenes from topical events all whizzing round within a revolving diamond shape. And it was once surveyed, by the industry's *Broadcast* magazine, to have a higher proportion of ABC 1 female viewers than any other programme on TV. In truth, that simply meant that, although the audience never reached more than two and a half million – not much bigger than Frost's – the viewers were mostly thinking women. And I was rightly proud of that at the time.

Presenting the programme was a happy time. It gave me the chance to interview the people who really interested me, at their most fascinating times. Everyone from David Owen, as he announced that he was leaving the SDP, to Nigel Kennedy, whose *Vivaldi's Four Seasons* album had hit Number One in the charts. And one programme was a live outside broadcast from the Berlin Wall, on the weekend it fell.

At home, life was splendid. My only other regular TV commitment was a Thursday afternoon programme on ITV called *TV Weekly*. Every Thursday I would leave our house in North London at six in the morning and travel to TVS in Southampton, returning about eight in the evening. It meant that I didn't see the children for a whole day, but compared to the lot of most working mums, it was perfect.

And then, during the summer, it became clear that my dream routine was about to be wrecked by a formidable force known as David Frost.

Frosty wanted his shows back – if not exactly all of them, he wanted the best dates. Which would inevitably leave me with the summer weekends – the so-called 'silly season', when there was always a dearth of journalistic stories and when the celebrities were away. So there was, for a topical programme, nothing very much to talk about, and no-one to talk to.

It was put to me in a variety of phrases, by a very awkward and embarrassed Bruce Gyngell, that I would have to do what I was told, because David Frost was a founder member of TV-am, and a Very Big Cheese indeed. I was also told that the company's board had discussed the matter, and that the directors had concluded that Frost would be better for them on the high-profile Sunday programme than I, because he could attract a greater amount of serious politicians. And that all the power of politics was needed to ensure that TV-am regain its franchise, coming up for renewal in the following year.

I was dumbfounded. The man who had been almost dismissive of Frost and his image just a few months before (and, significantly, half a world away from London) was now speaking a different, and almost deferential language. I pointed to the dates, phrases, promises in my contract. They would honour it as far as they could, Bruce promised. No-one was putting me on the streets – I would still get about fourteen or fifteen programmes to present, at some stage during the year. I had seen that stubborn look on Bruce's face when he was dealing with others, but never with me. It was almost like method acting – you just knew that it was not natural to him and he had perfected that steely stare in front of a mirror. It was method business behaviour – all the more cruel because he was working at it. And then he said something I'll never forget, because it completely betrayed the very real joy he had shown when I had become a mother.

'Those babies of yours cost us money,' he barbed. I muttered something in return about the fact that I'd been entitled under my contract to full maternity rights, and that I'd taken hardly any leave at all. But it was pointless. He'd hit me where it hurt.

And so it was over the next few weeks, while my *Diamond on Sunday* programme was being aired, live, every weekend, that Bruce became a stranger to me. Where once he would dart out of his glass office if he saw me walk past, to engage me in conversation, he would stay behind his desk, raising his papers to avoid eye contact. He had used to pop into my office for a chat, to ask how the children were, or to tell me about his. But now my office was quiet. It was the lull before the storm – because, pretty soon, he started to communicate by memo, or – worse still– by allowing his junior ministers to send me memos.

We had always prided ourselves, since the very beginning of the TV-am era, that we had almost invented a new kind of TV current affairs – based on an interview technique which defied the coldness and confrontational style of TV journalists like Brian Walden or Jeremy Paxman. We called it sofa television – and in its way it was every bit as dangerous as *Weekend World* or *Newsnight*, because many interviewees could be easily caught off-guard, relaxing into the cushions, the coffee and apparently easy chat, only to be floored by a simple but incisive question. Nick Owen and I had worked hard at perfecting the technique, over years of early morning interviews with mining boss Arthur Scargill, party leaders David Steel and David Owen, Labour supremos Michael Foot and Neil Kinnock, any number of Margaret Thatcher's cohorts, one momentous exclusive with Princess Michael of Kent about her alleged SS father and a memorable knockabout with Denis Healey.

The great and the good had gained a firm respect for breakfast TV, in much the same way that they had become convinced, in the previous decade, of the importance of the *Jimmy Young Show* on Radio 2. Breakfast TV was how you got to the voters – but it wasn't the 'easy ride' it somehow pretended to be. One slip-up, and you were headline news.

So I was shocked to receive, as my star within the political firmament of TV-am started to flicker, a memo from the Head of News, telling me that there would be serious repercussions if I was ever seen again on air, holding a TV-am coffee cup in the middle of an interview. Even if that exchange was merely with another TV-am journalist. (I had, in fact, been holding a cup while talking to our correspondent, Martin Frizell, who was doing a live broadcast from outside Strangeways Prison, where the inmates had been rioting the night before.)

It wasn't the cup which was important, of course. What was

significant was that the Head of News, Bill Ludford – a man who had been brought in to TV-am by my husband Mike because we had both thought so much of him – felt he could now write me stupid, petty memos. That in itself meant that my days at TV-am, the company I loved so much and for which I had worked long, dedicated and hellishly antisocial hours, were numbered. You can tell these things when your mini-fridge disappears overnight from your office – and mysteriously re-materializes behind the desk of some junior executive who was still at school when you made your first appearance on breakfast TV.

I went to my agent, who went to a lawyer, who went to a barrister. I decided that I wouldn't give in to TV-am's drastic alteration of my working schedule without a fight. And, contractually, right was very much on my side – though it was interesting to note that, by the time I had received the contract in Australia, many of the phrases which would have further protected my position had been uncannily left out.

You'll remember, though, that on that sunny morning on Kerry Packer's verandah overlooking Palm Beach, Bruce had had the sense to write down his promises. I still had that piece of paper. Maybe, although he couldn't admit it, he had been looking after me all along, as best he could. I like to think so. But there was no avoiding confrontation – and in the end, my agent, Jon Roseman, and I agreed to a showdown meeting, with Bill Ludford and TV-am's lawyer, Paul Vickers.

Not since the earliest days of that television station, when the likes of Anna Ford and Angela Rippon were fired, had there been such a high-profile, emotive showdown. But Bruce chose to delegate the unpleasantness to Bill. Show-business was not Bill's strong point – he was generally a man of few words, a red-wine-and-curry man, an ex-Fleet Street hack with a flair for news instinct rather than man-management. Woman-management was possibly his greatest weakness. The company had lost several talented girl presenters, notably after

13

confrontations with Bill. I always thought that, like a great many male executives in the world of TV, Bill seemed happier with female employees when they were in a junior position, and eager to please. Once they were rewarded with any degree of authority or position of power, he appeared less comfortable, and it was only a matter of time before they left, amid whispers that they had become too difficult, too demanding, too big-headed.

Strong women in TV are generally unloved. You'll find that many of the big female names have, on the face of it, bad or difficult reputations. But scratch the surface, and you'll inevitably discover that those bitching about them are the insecure, anonymous men whose simple lack of talent ensures that they remain unknown.

And so it was that, while still turning up for work every weekend, and enjoying great camaraderie with my small and loyal team, I issued a writ against TV-am for breach of contract.

It was an extraordinary situation. On Friday and Saturday afternoons, I would walk through the rotating glass door (with the little buttons on it which you were meant to press to promote inner peace and communal spirit – a Bruce Gyngellism), up the central staircase, and endeavour to find my office. It kept being moved, further and further away from Bruce's. Other employees didn't know whether they should even acknowledge me. The secretaries, parked obediently outside each executive suite, shot me sympathetic half-smiles. But mostly, people buried themselves in their work. I hadn't had much time to get to know the weekend workers. It was the army of journalists, producers, directors and researchers who worked on the main weekday programme that I knew best. They phoned in their support to my home phone. There were even two private calls from directors of the TV-am board, incredulous at what had been allowed to happen.

Indeed, my writ had made headline news – but it was,

ironically, a favourite adage of David Frost's which I decided to stick to during those uncomfortable days, when newspaper reporters tried every trick in their repertoire to get me to talk: 'Never complain, never explain.' And, by and large, though it was terribly tempting to put my point of view publicly, I managed to say very little about why I was suing TV-am.

Many of the papers made up their own reasons, and there were several stories about 'the worm turning' on the TV company which had made her a star. Some of the nastier writers made the ridiculously simplistic deduction that I wanted to be on TV all the time. One cartoon showed my face as the ever-present TV-am clock-face, in the corner of David Frost's show. 'There,' a viewer remarks, 'that should keep her happy!'

No-one thought, at least in print, that it was merely a case of a company going back on its word. Or of the younger, female, TV presenter losing out to the muscle of the older male. And throughout the whole nasty business, David Frost himself made no comment, no appearance nor involvement. So to this day, I could conclude that he, personally, knew nothing of it. I could... On the other hand, I remember that in 1983, when the station nearly folded just weeks after its launch, Frost took himself off to America while his fellow founder members of TV-am, Anna and Angela, were fired. He then calmly sent Anna Ford a plant – which she threw on to the compost heap where, typically, it thrived as if to mock her!

The horrible letters continued between their lawyers and mine. And it was clear that I would never return to work at TV-am. It was, therefore, a question of how much money they owed me, from a contract which they had failed to honour. It was now up to the lawyers. I was sure I had right on my side, but that doesn't stop you sweating when your solicitor rings up every so often with their latest unkind retort – and his latest estimate of how the legal fees are totting up.

The only good news on the horizon was that ITV had decided to commission a show which I had piloted for TVS, under the command of an old friend, Chris Riley. Chris was a wiry, hyperactive talent – he'd been a teacher, appeared with his mum on *The Generation Game* and got the TV bug. Just a few years later, he'd become one of the brightest TV producers in the industry. I met him at TV-am, where he was an Editor of the Day. His programmes were always fast and furious – bordering on mayhem – but well constructed and fun to present. And he had an instinct – one I've found to be surprisingly rare – for knowing how to handle TV performers, and give them the help and support they need.

Chris was now working for TVS in Southampton, having got fed up with the exhausting overnight shifts, and exasperated with Bruce, a boss with whom he couldn't reason. He'd formatted a TV show about television, a mixture of entertainment gossip, production news and behind-the scenes location filming. He'd contacted me while I was in Australia to ask if I would present the pilot.

I was only too happy to be involved – and thrilled when it was successful. Presenting *TV Weekly* would involve me in one long day's work a week. Combined with my TV-am weekend work, it was a perfect schedule for a new mother, who still wanted plenty of time to be with her children. Oliver, the elder of our two sons, was just three and starting nursery school. Jamie was hardly a toddler. They were every bit as challenging, rewarding and draining as I had expected children would be. But back in my carefree, single, childless days, I had never dreamed that I would want to be with them so much that I almost resented having to go to work.

I'd found what many mums dream of – a highly paid, challenging job, with hours that suited me and the kids. But as the legal wrangling dragged on through the late summer weeks, I started to get cold feet about the money this lawsuit was costing. And I was almost too busy, too preoccupied, too tense about things to notice that my period was late. Very late indeed. But once I thought about it, I just knew: 'Cyprus!'

I rushed to the calendar, tore it down and flicked back to July, where the word 'AWAY' was written large in black felt-tip. I did my sums. Yes, it was entirely possible that I was six weeks pregnant. How would I tell Mike? Another baby was the last thing we wanted right now. In fact another baby was the last thing we wanted full stop. Oliver and Jamie were quite enough, thank you. We'd never have planned a third.

Why is it that we women so often feel guilty when it comes to breaking the news about a surprise baby? Why do we feel as if we should apologize for the bombshell? After all, it takes two to make a child.... Armed with that thought, I slipped the newsflash in between courses at dinner that evening. Mike nearly choked. 'But how?' he spluttered.

'Cyprus...' I said. 'Don't you remember...'

'The lost baggage...' he recalled. 'But that was just once. No-one gets pregnant that easily....'

So that was it – no champagne, no fireworks. No ringing around our families to tell them they were going to be grand-parents again. We were having a baby – but neither of us was happy about it. We were both surprisingly silent. Mike smiled ironically, turned to me and said, 'What are we going to do about it?'

I shrugged my shoulders. 'I dunno....'

It was almost too big a subject to go into that night. We'd both had enough of a shock just taking in the facts. We were two people who'd always been very much in control of their lives. Until now.

'I suppose I ought to confirm it first....'

So I rang my girlfriend, Shirley. When you're well known – and particularly when you're tabloid newspaper fodder – you just cannot pop into Boots and buy yourself a pregnancy testing kit. It would be asking for trouble. And if your husband is pretty well known, too, you can't get him to buy one, either. Next morning I left the children with our nanny, Alex, and dashed round to my friend's flat. Shirley and I had been best friends since we were little. We'd shared everything together. Now we sat like secretive schoolgirls on the floor of Shirley's bathroom, staring at the test tube and waiting for the indicator paper to change colour.

Blue. There was no doubt about it now. Oh, my God, I was pregnant again. Shirley threw her arms around me – but I was weeping with panic, not delight. 'Oh, what am I going to do?' I wailed.

Shirley was shocked. She couldn't have children – and here was I, newly married with two adorable sons and moaning about adding to that joy. But you only know if you've been there yourself, how after two births in fairly quick succession you have to fight hard to recover. I was only just beginning, physically, to feel normal again after Jamie's birth. I had ballooned in size, followed and failed one diet after another to regain my figure, but at last, after hiring a highly expensive personal trainer, I had slimmed down to my normal nine stone. Jamie was only just getting the hang of sleeping through the night. From birth he'd been colicky and even at night he would wake every twenty minutes – reducing Mike and me to zombies.

I was scared about cot death – a colleague at TV-am had lost her baby daughter that way – so I had insisted on attaching Jamie to an apnoea monitor. It was a square-shaped sensor pad which you put underneath the child's mattress – and the alarm goes off if the baby stops breathing. I'd heard about these monitors from our GP, Peter Wheeler. He'd recently attended a family who'd had a cot death. He was profoundly shaken by the experience, and had told me all about the horror of what had happened that morning, when the family nanny had found the child dead. To make things worse, the parents were abroad, and had to be contacted by relatives who were all frantic with shock and grief.

I asked Peter what caused cot death. I didn't know very much about it, though I'd done at least two interviews about it on TV-am. One with the *Dr Who* actor, Colin Baker, whose son had been a cot death victim.

'They just don't know,' he said, sadly. 'The babies just seem to forget to breathe....'

The baby who had died had been one of twins – and they had had to put the other twin on constant surveillance, and a monitor. So, when I was expecting Jamie, I went back to Peter, and demanded that he tell me how to buy a monitor.

'But what would you do if the alarm went off?' he'd asked.

'I don't know – pick the baby up and shake him, I suppose,' I offered. The truth was, I hadn't even countenanced that it *would* go off. If cot death was caused by a baby forgetting to breathe, then I would simply remind it. At least that was better than finding your baby dead hours later.

So I got my monitor – and I used it, without being specially trained. No-one told me that some models were prone to go off all the time – and this one seemed to wait until Jamie was peacefully asleep and you had gone down three flights of stairs. Then, as your foot touched the last step, or you'd just made yourself a cup of tea, you would hear the shrill screech of the alarm – your heart would miss a beat, and you would race back up all those stairs again, dreading that your precious child was dying. When you got to his room, Jamie would be shaking with fright at the noise, and it would take another half hour to get him off. It drove us all nuts – and Lord knows what it did to the baby. Was every alarm a false one? Or did he stop breathing, only to be jerked back to consciousness by that devastating screech? I shall never know.

So when, months later, he was still waking ten or twelve times a night, I started to worry that he might be ill. Luckily, I had a friend who was a paediatrician at University College Hospital. I begged my first favour – and he invited Mike and me down to his unit in London's West End. 'Come on Thursday afternoon,' he said. 'It's usually pretty quiet then – that's when I do my bereavement clinic....'

19

As we were ushered down the corridor by a nurse, I remember noting that it was so very quiet it was almost sinister – even though there were treatment rooms and a large waiting area stacked with toys. And then, sadly, I remembered what he'd said about it being the time for his bereavement clinic. How sad, I thought, that as a paediatrician he doesn't only save little lives. He has to deal with death like any other doctor....

Did our baby have a problem? He gave Jamie a thorough check-up. 'No,' he concluded. 'But you two have. You both look tired. Tell me exactly what you do with Jamie at night. Because I'll bet a pound to a penny it's nothing to do with his health – it's more likely behavioural.'

He smiled sagely when I mentioned the apnoea alarm. 'But what would you do anyway if you found he wasn't breathing?'

'Shake him?' I tried.

'Look,' he said, sitting back. 'If you take my advice, you'll take the monitor off him and put it away in a cupboard.'

So we did. I'd become convinced myself that the wretched machine was wrecking our lives – I just hadn't found the courage to stop using it, afraid that Jamie might die without it. And it worked. I put the monitor away – and within days, Jamie was sleeping for longer periods. Soon, he was sleeping right through. We never looked back.

Like I said, everything at home was getting better. Oliver was starting nursery school – and we had found a brilliant new nanny, in whom I was gaining more and more trust. She was called Alex, and the kids adored her. That meant I could go to work without feeling guilty. We could go out in the evenings again, without worrying. Mike and I were just starting to feel like a couple again, rather than a pair of over-exhausted babysitters. That was why another baby seemed like bad news. We agreed to decide the fate of this next pregnancy over dinner at one of our favourite restaurants, Mosimann's.

It seems odd now, looking back, that we should go somewhere so plush, so luxurious, so romantic, to discuss such a thing. And, indeed, romance was very much on our minds. Though neither of us treated the subject of abortion lightly, we weren't so much discussing a baby's life as the survival of our marriage and our family. We both knew our partnership had been through a great deal of stress. We both understood the danger of yet more.

By the end of the evening I knew what I wanted to do. And Mike agreed. We took what we thought was the most sensible decision for the four of us. We would go for an abortion.

I am so very, very glad that I just couldn't go through with it.

Chapter 2

We had a smashing playroom in our London house. It was down in the basement, next to the kitchen. It had a frightful red carpet, and was dominated by a monstrous red velvet sofa – both of which we'd inherited from the previous owners. When they lived there, the woodwork was painted red, too – and the wallpaper was dark. I remember that when we'd first looked around the house, and gone down the stairway to the basement, it had seemed like descending into the flames of hell.

But we couldn't afford to change everything straight away – so we painted all the woodwork bright white, and washed the walls with primrose yellow. Suddenly it looked like a delightfully colourful children's room – and that's the way it stayed. Eventually it gathered adult clutter, too, like the fax machine, the satellite system, the video and the music centre, and so it became the heart of the house – and it always seemed to be bursting with children.

When you live in London, and you have a nanny, your house becomes part of the nanny circuit – which means that your kitchen is always alive with girls drinking coffee, organizing tea parties and outings for your youngsters. At three and eighteen months, our children had a far more active social life than us. They were always visiting the zoo, going on open-top bus rides around London, feeding the ducks in Regent's Park or seeing Postman Pat at the theatre.

This is a home which welcomes children, I thought one morning, as I was listening to them play in the garden. How could we reject one now? Slowly but surely, the little baby forming inside me was triggering hormones which were changing my mind. He was determined to be born.

Well! If I was going to have another baby, go through more bouts of morning sickness, lose my figure all over again, get all over-emotional again – then could I really cope with the legal mess I'd got myself into at work? For some time, Mike and I had wondered if we should now stop the legal proceedings. It was fast turning into one of those situations where both sides lose out and only the lawyers get rich. Like a divorce.

Mike was usually the one to insist on fighting injustice to the bitter end. In the past, he'd issued libel writs against newspapers – and continued the battle long after I would have backed away. In the face of horrendous newspaper threats, and even more vitriolic headlines, he'd had the temerity to dig his heels in. And, always, he'd been right to do so. But this time, even Mike felt that things had got out of hand. One morning, before he left for work at the satellite station, Music Box, where he was managing director, we had a shouting match about it. He said I'd been stupid to run up such a massive legal bill. It was clear TV-am were going to resist all the way, either out of spite, or to make me spend myself penniless.

I reluctantly picked up the phone to my lawyer, Ian Bloom, to tell him to back off – and to find a way to extricate me from the lawsuit and save as much money as possible. He wasn't in – his secretary promised he'd get back to me. Just two hours later, while I was changing Jamie's nappy and planning the children's lunch, Ian rang. He didn't wait to ask me why I'd phoned him. 'Great news!' he trumpeted. 'They've offered a settlement – and I think you're going to like it....'

I was to be paid every penny due in what was left of my two-year contract – and they didn't want me back to work for it. They must have thought I'd balk at that, since the original argument had been about airtime being taken from me. But in these new circumstances, the deal couldn't have been more suitable. Rather like a highly-paid, two-year term of maternity leave – albeit with no job waiting at the end of it. Still, I could live with that!

I rang Mike. 'My God, brilliant news,' he whistled. 'But you'd better get the deal sorted quickly – before they find out about the baby. Or they'll probably try and find all sorts of reasons to withdraw the offer....'

There was, also, the small matter of how my divorce from TV-am was to be announced. Tony Fitzpatrick, a long-time friend who ran his own public relations and press agency, advised that we talk to Bruce about how things might be done with dignity. 'After all,' he told me. 'You were the Queen of TV-am for six years. You can't just disappear into the night – especially when the press know that you were actually suing the buggers. You've got to say goodbye to your viewers properly.'

Mike and I laughed at the suggestion. We were sitting now in Tony's plush office in London's Docklands, furnished with plush black leather and chrome. He poured us champagne and handed round the Twiglets.

'Bruce will never let me back on that sofa!' I retorted.

'Don't be so sure,' wiled Tony. 'Bruce knows that you made that sofa famous. He knows how important it is to keep the audience happy – and he knows how fond those viewers are of you. 'You should be allowed to sit there, be given flowers, talk about how sad you are to leave – and then wave goodbye. Out of courtesy to your viewers.'

Mike and I shook our heads in unison. 'He'll never agree to it!' But Tony knew. He knew Bruce. His life partner, Jason Pollock, had been TV-am's show-business editor since the start of the station. They both knew Bruce almost as well as I – in some ways better.

And so, within days, Tony came back to us with the astonishing news that Bruce had agreed – and that I would be a guest on *Good Morning Britain* that very Friday. I would be able to say my goodbyes to the station I'd helped to build, and the viewers who'd liked, loathed and supported me since Day One.

I wore a black polo neck sweater, black pencil skirt, and my new Paul Costelloe red hunting jacket – an outfit I'd only recently slimmed into. But this morning I had to suck my tummy in. I daren't let them see what was already a less than flat stomach – or they might suspect.

Bruce had come to see me in the hospitality area, as I waited to go into the studio. 'You look fabulous,' he said. 'How are the children? And Mike?' And then he walked away, without waiting for my reply. I guess he felt awkward. But it made me sad that he seemed so cold.

So I went ahead with the niceties. Lorraine Kelly and Mike Morris, now the main presenters of my old show, did me proud – and were genuinely thrilled that I had been able to leave in style. As I left the building which had been my home from home for most of that decade, dubbed 'Egg Cup Towers' by the tabloid press, I felt it was the end of a wonderful period of my life. Bruce must have felt it too. He wrote me a note. It said:

And so we come to the end of an era. I cannot let it pass without writing to thank you personally for the great contribution you made to TV-am. Your dedication, commitment and professionalism was the hallmark of the time you spent with us. I do not underestimate the toll this took on your family life. I do want you to know how much we appreciated your presence.

Love Bruce

I owed a lot to that place and to the characters who'd peopled it but I'd also given a great deal, I hoped, towards its astonishing success. I would never forget it – and I can honestly say that I have never since worked anywhere so dangerous, exciting, so exhausting, and so very rewarding.

I felt I'd won a moral victory. I had made them honour their contract. Now I had things to do at home. After all, there was a new baby coming.

Chapter 3

One Monday morning, just as we were about to go on air with Frankie Howerd, the 'Oooooh! Missus!' comedian who was regularly brought on to the programme to cheer us all up, he turned to me and said sadly: 'You know, Anne, it's no fun being famous any more....' He'd just been savaged by the Sunday newspapers – and I remember thinking how terribly sad it was that his mood should match his celebrated hang-dog expression. After a lifetime of hard slog, working his way up the show-business ladder, and then a career spent making people laugh, did his talent really deserve to be rewarded with humiliating headlines and malicious words?

But the press in the Eighties were having a field day at the expense of anyone well-known. They were already regularly shredding Princess Diana's image with stories of anorexia; it seemed to the rest of us that one particular tabloid wouldn't be happy until they'd driven Elton John to suicide; and their alleged disclosures about *EastEnders* star Leslie Grantham made Frankie Howerd's moan appear sadly prophetic.

And, since I had 'risen from nowhere' on this precocious and notorious breakfast TV station, I automatically became press fodder. Everything I did seemed to make news. Even when I broke my toe one morning, bashing it on my briefcase on the way into work, it resulted in a story on the front page of the *Sun*. That was one of the few times in those days that they wrote anything nice about me.

Pressmen say that the public 'want to know' about celebrities' private lives – and that's how they sought to defend their most appalling tactics. On several occasions, I had reporters posing as policemen, delivery men, florists, and even doctors – just to get inside my front door. And it's very frightening. One started rifling through my dustbin – what on earth could he have been looking for?

The pressmen say you have to put up with it – it's part and parcel of being famous. And if you do nice interviews for *Hello!* magazine, you cannot moan about uninvited press intrusion. Well, I did once do a feature and photo spread for *Hello!* magazine in its early days – so I suppose I had it coming to me....

I was almost eaten alive by the press in those days. My worst enemy was the *Sun*, closely followed by the *News of the World* and the *People*. The other tabloids seemed to be fair and unfair in equal measure. But it was the journalists on Britain's best-selling popular paper who really went for my throat, with a determination that felt like deliberate destruction.

My biggest mistake was having a private life at all. My next mistake was having a less than conventional one. Unfortunately for my press image, I was already in love by the time my name hit the headlines. And my love was already married – to someone else. I don't seek to defend what some would still consider an indefensible situation. But sometimes life doesn't hand you everything on a clean plate. I'm not the first girl who has found herself hopelessly in love with the wrong person. And I certainly shall not be the last.

Whatever the rights and wrongs – as a human being, you need time to sort these things out. Time and privacy. But when you've got at least three newspaper reporters, photographers at their heels, standing on your doorstep – you have neither. Your own emotions, and the hurt and sensibilities of others – including children – take second place to the newsmen's 'right to publish'.

In effect, that means that when the man at the door is shouting through your letterbox 'Are you in love with Mike Hollingsworth or not?' you know that you cannot win either way. If you speak to them, you are fuelling their story. If you don't, they'll run with their own version and defend their inaccuracies by citing your unwillingness to co-operate. If you go to the door, they'll snap you looking strained, worn and defeated. Unless, that is, you make yourself up, in which case you'll be described as looking brazen. So you don't answer the door at all – in which case they use a file picture of you, smiling all over your face. Whatever happens, tomorrow's headlines will only make the private anguish worse, on all sides.

But the real malice which they reserved for me dated back to one incident over which I felt I had no control. Mike and I were very much together – though he was not yet divorced – when I found I was pregnant with our first baby. We decided that this was a baby we very much wanted. My GP, Peter Wheeler, was delighted for me. But he advised me to wait until I was at least twelve weeks pregnant before telling anyone. As we all know with babies, you can never be absolutely sure that all will go well in the first few weeks.

Mike and I hadn't even thought how we would break the news to our respective families, when I thought I was miscarrying. It was almost Christmas, and we were just about to go shopping in Harrods one evening. As I walked up the steps to the Hans Crescent entrance, I collapsed on Mike's arm, bleeding heavily. Luckily we were only steps from the car, and just half a minute from Peter Wheeler's surgery. He was there as I staggered in. By this time I was in tears, and both Mike and I were panicking at the thought of losing the baby. Peter arranged for me to have an immediate ultrasound scan at a nearby private hospital – and, within the hour, we were relieved and comforted to see the little blip on the scanner screen which showed that Oliver was still alive. I had a placenta praevia. I had to go home, put my feet up for a few days and rest – or we could still lose the baby.

We'd been home just a few hours when the phone rang. It was a reporter from the *News of the World*. They had been tipped off that I was pregnant. Could I please confirm or deny?

31

I was stunned. How could they possibly know? I hadn't even told my parents yet. And anyway, I couldn't safely think that I was pregnant. I could still have a miscarriage.

The reporter must have sensed my shock. 'We have very good sources,' he said, contemptuously. 'We know it's true.'

'You can't possibly know,' I stumbled.

'Well, are you pregnant, or not?'

I hesitated, and then plumped for it: 'No,' I said, and put the phone down.

Later that evening, the TV-am press officer rang us to tell us that they, too, had received a call from the *News of the World*. They were going to run a story all over their front page with a headline saying 'Baby for TV Anne' and the first line of the story: 'Anne Diamond last night denied reports that she is pregnant. But....'

No time, nor privacy to even consider the little baby inside me – nor how we were going to cope, whether we would marry, where we would live. The most important thing at that moment was ringing round the family – so that they wouldn't read it in the papers first.

Little did I know that, from that day onwards, the *News of the World* and its associated papers would never forgive me for denying what they saw as a true story. Several times later in my history with them, they would brand me 'Liar'. The press in the UK has altogether curious double standards. On the one hand, they pester you to do interviews and photo shoots with them. Then they decry people who seek publicity.

It's difficult now to understand the media interest I attracted when my pregnancy was first confirmed. It's an extraordinary thing, but even in the modern 1980s, it was unprecedented for a woman to be on TV, as regularly as every day, while she was pregnant. Women simply shied away from the camera during the fat months. Most jobs in the TV world would allow you to do just that. But I couldn't take five or six months off. And, anyway, I didn't want to. So I, unwittingly, became the first female presenter in the UK to be on air, live every morning, throughout the pregnancy. Some critics later described me as 'flaunting my pregnancy'. I didn't. Actually, I refrained as much as I could from mentioning it. But mums-in-waiting up and down the country wrote to me, saying they were going through exactly the same experience.

On the day it was announced, Michael Aspel was our guest. He made a huge fuss of me – and later talked about me in the introduction of his prime-time talk show. Jasper Carrott, too, made me his first gag that night in his show. And Terry Wogan invited me on to his chat show to talk about it.

So, on the night I went into labour, Mike wasn't surprised to learn that, while we were still in the delivery room, the press had been tipped off that the baby was about to arrive. And they all wanted a photograph.

We sent out a message, via the hospital's administrators, that mother and baby were doing fine, but that we would not be doing any interviews or photocalls for a few days at least. But for one particular publication that was not good enough. I was still drinking tea, and looking forward to a bath, Mike holding the baby, when the matron knocked on our door and came in.

'I just thought I should warn you,' she said. 'I don't want to alarm you – but our porters have just had to deal with a man who was found wandering down the corridor looking for you. He was dressed in a white coat and was pretending to be a doctor. He was apparently from the *Sun*....'

And that was why, just six hours after I'd given birth, Mike, Oliver and I went home. We were smuggled out of the hospital via the service lift and in a laundry van. Once we were in our own car, we made for home. But our own entrance was surrounded by pressmen, so we went into the adjoining block of flats, up to the roof, and walked across the roof and down the stairs to our own flat. When I look back on it now, I go weak at the knees, but we'd have done almost anything then for a few days' absolute privacy.

Once the press realized we were inside, they pushed letters through our letterbox, pleading and offering money for exclusive first shots of the baby. The *News of the World* sent a big bouquet and a letter bidding £50,000. 'I'll bet there's a bug in these flowers,' I laughed, as I arranged them. And then I grew cautious. In those days, it was entirely possible that they could have bugged them. 'How would you like them, Kitty?' I asked my housekeeper, a dear old lady who was married to the caretaker of the flats. 'Why don't you take them home?'

Kitty gave them a peremptory glance. 'Well, they're too good to waste – but I'm not taking them home so's the papers can listen in to me and my Les. I'll take them to the church. And then if the *News of the World* are listening in, all they'll get is hymns.'

Every time a florist arrived with a new bouquet, the waiting reporters would rush at the door, cameras already flashing. Several beautiful posies got squashed because we were too afraid to open the door further than the security chain would allow it. One reporter, from the *Today* newspaper, offered the florist £15,000 if she could snatch a Polaroid snapshot of the baby.

When we eventually did agree for shots of Oliver to be printed in the *Daily Star* we were accused of hawking our son around Fleet Street in order to make money. This is rubbish – but the other newspapers printed the accusation so often, it became perceived as being true. Even *Spitting Image*, the satirical puppet programme, featured me in a sketch. I was seen pushing a supermarket trolley, with Oliver in the baby seat. When I got to the till, and the checkout girl asked for money, I got out a Polaroid camera, took a picture of Ollie – and paid for the shopping with it!

Then, of course, they went for our nanny....

Debbie had come to us from her last job as a nurse at

London's famous Great Ormond Street hospital for children. She'd written to me at TV-am – a lovely letter saying that she'd like to look after a healthy child after so many years nursing sick ones. First she was interviewed by my lovely loyal secretary, Gay – who was a mum herself and knew the ropes of working motherhood – and then she came to see me. I liked her straight away. Her experience with babies was fantastic – but her ability to whip together a tasty Caesar salad and her skill at mixing a gin and tonic made her outstanding!

I thought we'd got it right with Debbie. But what I forgot – or rather, I didn't know it would be significant – was that Debbie's training was as a nurse, not a nanny. Mike and I began to feel that we were being treated like unwelcome visitors – and that Ollie was a patient. He was always spotlessly clean, well turned out, routinely aired in his pram, and promptly put to bed in his own room. But we never felt that he was a member of the family. In fact, we started to feel that we were all outsiders in an efficiently run ward.

One morning I'd popped out to Mothercare and come back home with a baby carrier – one of those sling things which you tie in unfathomable knots around your body, and which holds your baby against your chest in a papoose. 'Look, just what we need for carrying Ollie around the house!' I said proudly, as I unwrapped it. 'Now, how does it go?' I looked to Debbie for help.

She took the carrier from me, slipped it around her shoulders and waist, popped the baby into it and looked up, smiling. 'That's great!' she smiled, and then at Oliver: 'You like that, don't you?'

I stood there , looking at the nanny wearing my baby. I had bought the carrier for me, not her – and I was reduced to looking on, rather like a visitor who'd brought a gift for a new mum and baby. In one insensitive, uncaring gesture, she had robbed me of a simple delight.

What's more, as the end of my eight weeks maternity leave

loomed, Debbie was licking her lips at the prospect of my return to work. She even admitted to it, when we had our upsetting but inevitable 'little chat'. We agreed that it wasn't working, and that she would leave as soon as she could. She said she needed to go off and arrange things. I thought she meant she was looking for another job, or somewhere to stay. I was glad she had taken it so well – and I hoped we would be able to remain friends. It was still morning, and I fed Ollie and played with him until he fell asleep on my bed. For once, Debbie wouldn't fly in and whisk him away to be tucked neatly into the crisp white sheets of his own cot.

It was probably about three hours later that I got the phone call.

'Hello – is that Anne Diamond? It's Kevin O'Sullivan, from the *Sun*.'

My stomach churned. It always did when one of those guys rang. And how had he found our phone number? But I'd had brushes with this one in the past. He was a well-known Fleet Street terrier. Once he had his teeth into you, there was no letting go. What on earth could he want?

'I just thought you'd like to know, Anne, that I've just had lunch with your nanny. She's told me a lot of very interesting things... How do you feel about that?'

There were no words to describe it. After a short silence, thankfully I went on to automatic pilot. It's something I had come to learn – before you say anything you may later regret, you should always buy yourself time. And it's always better than slamming the phone down, because that gets reported, too, as a sign of horror or hostility.

'Can I get back to you?' I stammered, trying to sound cool.

'Please do,' he cooed, and then gave me his number. But I didn't phone him back – I called Mike. By now, my heart was beating fast. Surely not our most private moments with our wonderful new baby, surely not our intimate thoughts – shared with a trusted employee – surely not our personal family

36

photographs all over pages of the *Sun*? Surely she hadn't dealt us such a betrayal?

'Get Shirley to come over and be with you,' advised Mike, always organized even in the most prickly predicament. 'I'll be with the lawyers most of the afternoon.'

Sure enough, Shirley dropped what she was doing and rushed around – though she could barely believe what had happened. While we were sitting in my living-room, still in shock and trying to drink tea, I heard the key in the lock of the front door. It was Debbie. She made straight for her room, but I followed her, and asked her in as calm a voice as I could muster why she had done it, though a lump kept coming to my throat. She was stuffing clothes and personal belongings into a black plastic bin bag. Others – already stuffed – were by the door.

She couldn't look at me – she just muttered: 'I've got nothing to say....' I remember thinking immediately that it was an odd sort of thing to state. It was a phrase well used by people familiar with handling the press.

She shuffled her bin bags out of the door – and left on the hall table the door keys and the two credit cards which she used on my account at Mothercare and Marks & Spencers. Limply, I watched her go. She'd performed her exit quite well.

I rang Mike again – and got him on his mobile phone. He was sitting in a lawyer's office. 'Debbie's just come back and taken her things away,' I whimpered. 'She wouldn't listen to anything I had to say....'

Mike mumbled a few hurried words to the lawyers at his side and then came back with: 'Go after her, and ask her to retract. It's worth a try....'

I looked outside. Debbie was packing the bags into a car, being driven by a man I thought could be her brother. I rushed out, and immediately became aware that a photographer was standing on the opposite pavement – snapping me as I hurried towards Debbie. Was he there to catch me throwing an hysterical tantrum? Was he after shots of a cat-fight?

By now, Debbie was in the front passenger seat. 'Debbie, please – don't do this,' I entreated. 'Even if you want to hurt me and Mike, don't betray little Ollie. I thought you really cared for him....'

She looked up at me – this time right in my eyes. I could see that she was confused and upset. 'Don't worry,' she snapped. 'I haven't said anything horrible about you. I'm not even sure I'm going to go ahead with it anyway.'

With that, the car pulled away. I turned back to the door-way. The photographer was snapping away, but I resisted the temptation to throw something at him. That would have made a great picture.

Mike spent most of the night at the lawyers. They had eventually been forced to contact a judge in chambers who had granted an injunction, ordering the *Sun* to stop the story. Their presses were already rolling – and it was almost unheard of to stop them once they were printing. It caused unbelievable mayhem at the *Sun* – and they weren't to forgive us for it.

Debbie rang later in the evening. She was sorry. She told me the reporter, Kevin, had met her in a pub, and offered her £30,000 in cash for her story. 'That's more than most people earn in a year,' she gasped at me. I could almost see her point.

'So did you agree to tell them anything – did you sign anything?' I asked her.

'They said I'll get the money later....'

'But did you tell them anything?' I asked again.

'Well, he did get out his notebook and write down quite a lot,' she admitted. 'But I'm sure they won't print anything if I ask them not to....'

Well, that's what you might think, if you'd never handled the press before.... 'Oh, Debbie,' I sighed. 'Don't you see? You've already given them what they want. They'll simply open the quote marks and say what they like. And I'd be surprised if you ever get your money, either.'

She went silent at the other end of the phone. And then she promised: 'I'll phone them and tell them I don't want anything to do with it....'

An hour later she rang again, this time in tears. They had more or less told her to get stuffed. They had their story, she said, and claimed they had never discussed money.

Of course, the *Sun* had lawyers as wily as their journalists. They could not print the story in the *Sun*, so the magnates at News International decided to print it in *Today*, a sister publication. Debbie had said some pretty hurtful things. Like how I apparently treated Oliver like a new toy. How I was terrified he would be kidnapped. How Mike and I argued – and how he was annoyed by the baby crying. To me, the real hurt was the fact that she'd gone to the newspapers at all. If you read it, you could quickly see that she was merely describing the private tensions which must happen in any family when the first baby arrives. Maybe she was surprised that life at home with a TV couple wasn't more like the *Mary Tyler Moore Show*.

(A year and a half later, Debbie died. Although a trained nurse – and a skilled one according to her nursing qualifications – she had succumbed to an eating disorder and had destroyed herself through massive laxative abuse. Of course, because she had once made headlines, the press reported her death, and the coroner's inquest findings – something which must have been dreadfully hard for her family to bear. And I apologize to her relatives if mentioning her here has added to their grief. But I think that she, too, was a victim of the press's misguided belief that any information, however private and confidential, was theirs to print.)

I hadn't even got back to work yet – and both Mike and I started to doubt whether we'd ever find a nanny we could trust. But we had good friends. Shirley was thrilled to help – and luckily, she had some time free. She relished looking after Oliver, but it couldn't be permanent. And neither Mike nor I felt we could trust another outsider. That's when Paula Yates stepped in with a unique gesture.

We'd known each other on and off for some time – mostly because we had come to know Bob Geldof, Paula's rock star husband. He'd appeared on TV-am many times during the making of the Band Aid record, to raise funds for famine victims in Ethiopia. Bob had planned, as a follow-up, a live version of the phenomenon – he planned to call it Live Aid, and to have it broadcast live throughout the world. It had sounded impossibly ambitious to us in the television industry. Getting TV companies in Britain to agree to do anything simultaneously was nearly impossible – let alone his dream of reaching the entire world. But he was a fascinating man – and he might just do it. So Mike, who was then the Director of Programmes at TV-am, agreed to support him as much as he could – and the company agreed to send Bob, with a film crew and me as a reporter, to Ethiopia, to see for himself what needed to be done, and how the charity money could be best spent.

As a result we came to see more and more of Bob and Paula socially. They were a close family – at that time they had just one daughter, the notoriously named Fifi Trixiebell. But it was clear they wanted more. We had been with them, in fact, on the very day I went into labour. Bob had been stuck for a celebrity to open the fête which was held annually at his Kent mansion, and he'd asked me if I would help out. I was so bored with waiting for the baby to come, that I agreed. By my reckoning, I was almost nine and a half months pregnant. When I look back at the photos now – I don't know how I even had the nerve to go out, let alone be photographed at a public event. Even more amazing was the fact that I wasn't jostled into labour by the journey along country roads to their house, by the intense heat, or by the wonderful summer pudding Paula had made for tea. Or maybe I was – because by the time we headed for bed that night, my head hit the pillow and my waters immediately broke.

So now Paula's act of friendship came as a welcome act of Live Aid. 'I've thought about it, and there's only one thing which would be truly useful to you right now,' she said.

'Yee-e-e-es?' I wondered.

'I'm going to lend you my nanny for a while. She's been with us for ages – she's fantastic – and she'll get you all sorted out. But mind – I want her back. OK?'

Now Paula's nanny was legendary. She was called Anita, and she strode into our home with a sense of purpose and confidence that restored our faith in human nature, and, in particular, the belief that we might find someone who would look after our child, fit into the family, and become the godsend which Anita was to the Geldofs. 'Give me time – and I'll find you the nanny of your dreams,' she told us and proceeded to interview us about the nanny we would like to have – what sort of people we were at home and what our expectations were of life, and of our child. She stayed with us a couple of weeks – and showed me what it was truly like to have the best in professional child care. I'll never forget her's – or Paula's – kindness.

Anita couldn't find anyone for us straight away – but I'd been lucky. Nanny Sue walked into our lives at just the right moment, though she only stayed with us six months. She was from the famous Norland College – but more importantly, she was the daughter of old friends of mine. Her mother and father had been stalwart members of my home town's operatic society, where I'd been an ambitious junior. Tom and Sally Rollins were the nicest of people, and thoroughly down-to-earth. Their daughter could be nothing less – and here she was, applying for our job. She was a brilliant nanny, and Oliver was lucky to have her during those first few infant months. When she left us – as nannies do – I was bereft. I rang Paula's house – and spoke to Anita.

In the meantime, I hired Carol. Again, it just didn't work. I worked in breakfast TV. Carol didn't get in from her nightclubbing until the early hours – often just moments before I left for work. And once I heard her arrive by the crunching sound outside as the car bumpers hit the street bollards. When I got home, at about midday, the house would often be silent. I would gingerly go upstairs, wondering why. More often than not, Carol was fast asleep in bed, with Oliver, at nine months, still in his night-time sleepsuit, lying in her bed beside her, staring at the ceiling.

Carol and I agreed we were animals from different time zones. It was her boyfriend, whom I'd met for only thirty seconds at the front door, who sold his story to the *News of the World*. In it, among the other scathing remarks about how I expected nannies to be slaves, he said he'd never ever seen me change a nappy. That in itself was true. Like I said – thirty seconds at the front door was all I'd ever seen of him. But it rankled – the idea of me never changing a nappy. I would still like to sock him in the face with one.

Nanny Sue was on the phone that Sunday morning. 'Do you want me to ring up the newspapers and stand up for you?' she almost sobbed.

Just as Mike and I were seriously considering which one of us should now give up work, and become a house-parent – Anita rang. 'I've found you the nanny of your dreams!' she proclaimed.

And she had.

Anne Waterman wafted into our lives like a breath of fresh air. Oliver adored her – and we came to trust and love her. She came all over the world with us: she fell in love with Australia when we did, potty-trained in Los Angeles, wheeled a buggy around Manhattan, took Ollie on the rides in Disneyworld, and taught him to use chopsticks in Hong Kong. In Sydney, where we lived for three glorious months in a millionaire's house overlooking the Harbour Heads, she would take Oliver swimming or playing on the beach every morning before breakfast – while I nursed the newly-born Jamie. She was exactly what we needed. And when she left us – because, dammit, she fell in love – once more Anita helped us.

'I don't suppose you ever get two nannies of your dreams, do you?'

'Of course you do!' said Anita. 'I'll find you the next dream person.' And she did – Alex.

Alex came for her interview on a particularly difficult day. Oliver was being an obstreperous toddler – and Jamie had kept me up all night, and was now screaming for his latest bottle of milk. I was sitting in the upstairs living-room of our terraced house in North London. I thought it would look better than the *Steptoe and Son* junkyard downstairs. But Alex took half a minute to figure us out. She just sort of scooped up the children – and they were immediately captivated. Within fifteen minutes and over our third cup of tea, when the boys seemed more content and the atmosphere less frenetic, I knew Anita had done it again. Suffice it to say Alex is still with us. And every one of our children has been the better for knowing her.

Because if you cannot look after your children yourself all the time – and few of us can – then the person to whom you entrust that task must either be grandma, auntie – or otherwise a professional who's very special indeed. I simply cannot understand those who belittle the jobs of childminder, carer, nanny or teacher. To me, next to parenthood, those have to be the most important jobs of all.

Chapter 4

By contrast to the circus which surrounded Oliver's and Jamie's births, Sebastian's arrival was of little interest to the media. By then, we were married – and I had given up the high-profile business of broadcasting every day from TV-am. Indeed, my only TV committment was *TV Weekly*. The furore over my departure from TV-am had long ceased, and on the personal front, life had never been quieter nor more peaceful.

I had been invited to appear on a BBC morning programme about celebrities and their mums – and had chosen that as an opportunity to announce the pregnancy. It resulted in a single paragraph in the next day's papers: 'Baby Number Three for TV Anne'. 'My goodness, what a difference,' I thought. 'We must be respectable nowadays!' Oliver and Jamie were looking forward to having a baby brother. They had even given him a name – though we couldn't figure out exactly why they had decided to call my bump 'Supi'. At any rate, it stuck so firmly that, by the time his birth loomed near, our family were worried that we might actually christen him with that name. Eventually, we chose Sebastian with Patrick as his second name. I reasoned that if he ever needed to explain his nickname to anyone, he could say it was simply the running together of his two initials, S and P. So his nickname led to the choice of his real Christian names, rather than the other way round.

The pregnancy itself, however, was not particularly easy this time. Towards the end I had a condition known as poly-hydramnios – which means I had too much amniotic fluid – and I was uncomfortably large and breathless. Four weeks before Supi was due, I started to suffer from chronic backache.

Our nanny, Alex, reminded me she was going away to her grandmother's house in Devon that weekend. 'Perhaps I'd better stay,' she volunteered. 'Maybe you're going to have the baby sooner than you think....'

'No, there's another month to go yet,' I panted. 'Don't worry.'

'I don't want you going into labour while I'm away – I don't want to miss any of the action!' Alex laughed as she brought me a cup of tea that Saturday morning. I was still in bed. But the pain seemed better. Perhaps it had just been backache after all.

But Alex couldn't have been on the train more than half an hour when my twinges became painful – and I rang my obstetrician, Maggie Thom.

'You'd better come and see me.' She sounded worried. 'I'll meet you at the Wellington at ten.'

Mike rang Alex's best friend, Sandra, who was also a nanny but with a husband and child of her own. Could she pop around and mind the children while we went to the hospital?

'But where's Alex?' she asked.

'Hurtling towards Devon,' answered Mike. But Alex's family had already assured him they would turn her right round as soon as she arrived in Exeter. They knew she would want to be with us.

'Typical!' laughed Sandra – and she came round. Which was just as well, because I was well into premature labour.

It was not a painful labour – since by child number three Maggie Thom and I had agreed on the wonders of epidurals. But I did start to get worried when, much later into the evening, a paediatrician entered the room, and started kitting up the little special resuscitation trolley at the other end of the delivery room. Maggie caught my concern. 'It's just routine – because the baby's coming early,' she said.

My perfect little boy, our third son, our special Supi, was born shortly after five o'clock that Saturday evening. There was a lot of suctioning noise going on at the 'business end' of me – he wasn't placed straight on to my stomach, as the others had been. The paediatrican was busily doing something with him. The midwife wrapped him in a towel as they cleared his airways. Then they cut the cord.

'He's having a few small problems with his breathing – but nothing to worry about. It's just because he's a bit premature. But you can hold him for a few minutes.' They handed him to me. He had a pinky-grey little face, still covered in greasy vernix but unmistakably the likeness of his brothers. Mike took a quick snap with the camera. But the baby shot me a glance which smacked of panic – and then went quite blue. I turned to the midwife: 'He can't breathe!' and handed him back hurriedly. I was still being stitched up – and felt quite helpless while my little son was rushed to the warming unit again and more suction sounds began.

Mike hovered, sensing their concern. Our little boy was a good size, and appeared perfect. But he was definitely having problems with his breathing – and was struggling to live.

'We'll just take him to the special care baby unit for a few minutes,' they said, wheeling him away. 'Please don't worry – he just needs a bit of oxygen....'

The midwife came back a few minutes later. 'Don't worry – they'll just keep him for twenty minutes or so. Have a cup of tea, and try to relax – he's absolutely beautiful.'

Her next bulletin informed us that they might keep him in intensive care for a couple of hours. But again, nothing to worry about. I still couldn't walk, because of the epidural. So they wheeled me, flat on my back on a patient trolley, in through the doors of the special care baby unit to see him. Now he was washed – and quite pink – but laid out, flat on his back, like a laboratory specimen, under a warming light. There were wires to his chest and toes – and several machines were flashing red numbers and blipping green lights. He was almost encapsulated in a clear perspex hood, which had a long tube leading to an oxygen cylinder.

It was then I first realized that our little Supi was seriously ill. And – though he'd been the baby we hadn't expected and we'd joked that he would have to 'be a good baby' and he'd 'have to fit in with the rest of us and be no trouble' – his life was suddenly just as important as Oliver's and Jamie's. I didn't want him to die. I reached out my arm, and caressed the tiny heel of his dainty little foot – the only bit of him that wasn't under the oxygen box.

I felt unnervingly out of control. Here was I, helpless on a hospital trolley, drips still taped to my hand and arm, and there was my little child, pathetically clinging on to life, his chest almost collapsing with the effort of every breath. I wanted to grab him, and make a run for it. But instead I meekly listened to the professionals telling me not to worry, and wheeling me back to my own room.

I calmed down when Doctor Stanley Rom, the senior hospital paediatrician, came to visit. He had been called in to see Supi, and his manner was quiet and composed, almost soothing.

'Your little chap is not too well,' he started. Thank goodness he was not going to tell me not to worry. He could see I already was. 'He is having some problems breathing – and we're going to find out why. Now it could be that his oesophagus is incomplete, in which case we may have to talk about an operation. But we're going to have to do an X-ray first – to see what's happening.'

The champagne you always get at the Wellington with a new baby was waiting on ice. Mike had gone back home to organize Sandra, Alex (who had just returned from her day on the railways) and the boys – and he would be back soon.

The X-rays showed Supi's oesophagus was, thankfully, completely developed. They had been able to pass a tube into his lungs. There was nothing wrong with him that time, and careful nursing, wouldn't heal.

I had a bath, more tea and something to eat. And then one of the midwives offered to wheel me in a chair, around to the special care baby unit that was to become so familiar over the next two weeks. Because, although they had said Supi would be there at first for just twenty minutes, then two hours, then overnight, he would end up staying there for two weeks. And now I started the long process, as all parents do when they have babies in SCBU, of learning which tubes go where, and which machines do what.

'That one tells you his oxygen saturation,' the sister said. 'And that one is his heart rate.'

And all the time, while other little lives fought in incubators besides our own, I could not take my eyes off the little mite I already felt was part of our family, his little rib cage, puffing out bravely with each breath, and then collapsing so dramatically that I could have sworn I could almost see his spine through the skin. He was foaming slightly at the mouth – but his little arms and legs lay motionless. At the bonny weight of 5lb 13oz he was bigger than the other babies in SCBU – but he seemed to have worse breathing problems. Apparently that had something to do with my excess amniotic fluid.

I stared at him, gently stroking those little feet, until the sister thought I should get some rest myself. And, when Mike returned, I had a lot to tell him.

It was a lonely night, without my baby. The midwives kept popping in with bulletins – and I went to see him myself once, walking slowly along the corridor on legs still wobbly from the epidural. They said he was doing well. But he didn't look any different to me. His breathing still looked critical.

'Should he be here?' my husband asked Doctor Rom, in as tactful a manner as possible. 'Or should he be in a children's hospital, like Great Ormond Street?'

Dr Rom smiled wryly. He knew exactly what we meant. You book into a luxury hospital like the Wellington for just that – luxury. But when it comes to life and death – maybe the best place to be is down the road, at one of the big teaching hospitals in London.

'I understand what you're getting at, and yes,' he said, 'Sebastian needs to be where he'll get the finest medical care there is. If for one second I believe we should move him to another hospital, I will do just that. But right now I have absolute confidence that this hospital has everything he needs. You were right to ask. You love your little boy and you want the best for him. And I'll make sure he gets the very best.'

We started to relax. We visited Supi again. He still didn't look any better – but we began to understand that he needed time. He had been born too soon, and would have to go on 'cooking gently' inside the incubator instead of inside me. We couldn't hug him, cuddle him or welcome him properly into the world, because he hadn't really been born yet. The Special Care Baby Unit, dimly lit and quietly throbbing with machinery as it was, was almost like an extension of the womb. Only when he came out would he be properly with us.

Mike came again in the afternoon, this time with Alex and the boys. Sister Chan, whose meticulous manner I mistook at first for officiousness, allowed the boys in to see their brother, but barred Alex because she was not a blood relative. She stood outside the SCBU door, her eyes welling up with tears as she watched Oliver and Jamie walk in. At three years old and eighteen months, they could hardly understand that this tiny pink baby, whose face was all but obscured by tubes, was their little brother.

We stayed for a few minutes while they admired the machinery, Mike shot some video, and then we all headed back to my room, where we opened the champagne and drank a toast to Supi's health. The boys had made me some cards – and they had brought flowers.

Supi, meanwhile, was moved to a more permanent special care cot, and was laid out on his tummy, which helped his breathing. Not only did it make him more comfortable, but it wasn't so distressing to look at, since you couldn't see his sad little rib cage crumple with every respiration.

And so, over the next few days, new words appeared in our vocabulary – as they must with every parent who goes through the experience of having a child in special care. Words like 'Skiboo' and 'intubate' became commonplace. I learned how to change a nappy without dislodging the drips and sensors. I found that he loved having his spine gently stroked – his face would visibly relax. And I would discover that, after sitting for a while by his cot, caressing his little toes, or patting his bottom, hours would have passed by.

And, all around me, other babies were coming and going, their anxious parents running the full spectrum of human emotions. And I realized how very lucky we were.

Chapter 5

Anyone who was in the same maternity wing at the same time as me would remember me as the strange, almost obsessive person in a tartan dressing-gown, pushing a wheeled object up and down the corridor between my room and the Skiboo (the nickname for the Special Care Baby Unit).

Shrouded in a white blanket, its identity wouldn't have been immediately obvious to the outside world. It was the electric breast pump. This time I was determined to succeed at something I'd failed to do with my first two sons – breastfeeding. It was a skill that had passed me by when God had handed out natural talents. I'd seen – in fact I'd interviewed – all sorts of baby experts from Hugh Jolley to Michel Odent, extolling its virtues. I'd witnessed friends of mine – ex professional models with figures that could grace a catwalk just days after giving birth – almost drowning their gurgling offspring in cascades of milky goodness.... But me, with natural assets large enough to generously fill a 'medium' size Mothercare nursing bra, I couldn't produce enough to keep a fairy alive.

When they were new-born, both Oliver and Jamie had taken one look at me and opted for the Cannon Babysafe and SMA Gold. My breastfeeding history was a sorry tale of personal torture followed by guilt and tears. I'd had one-to-one tuition from a La Leche League counsellor and I'd tried the Sheila Kitzinger twenty-four-hour 'peak production plan'. But nothing worked.

When you write or say anything publicly about child care, you have to be seen to beat the drum for breastfeeding. And I know that breast is best – for everyone concerned. I accept that new research even suggests that it's positively beneficial for the mother, and could help reduce her risks of developing breast cancer.... But if you can't do it, you can't do it – and feeling guilty as hell doesn't help you or your baby.

But this time, I thought, I'd got help on my side. Supi could not make many demands on me, since he wasn't allowed any milk yet – and I was surrounded by a huge team of midwives, all of whom were trained in teaching women to breastfeed. If I cannot do it now, I thought, I never will. But because I couldn't even hold Supi yet, let alone put him to the breast, I did my best without him. I became intimate with the Skiboo breast pump.

Day five – and Dr Rom said that Supi could have his first milk. One millilitre – to be put down his nasal gastric tube, and siphoned into his stomach. They would then see how he reacted, and whether he could digest it properly. I went back to my room with a challenge. Could I produce one millilitre of milk? It's not a huge amount, by any standards, when you think that five millilitres fill a teaspoon. But it wasn't easy. Squeezing blood out of a stone would have been simpler. It must have taken half an hour – but I got there. A milky white drip of colostrum, a mother's first 'supermilk', hovered on the edge of the sterile feeding bottle which I'd brought with me.

The midwife looked at my offering, and giggled. 'Well, there's not much of it – but it's power-packed!' she said, taking it up into a syringe. 'Let's go and give it to him....'

Supi was doing well. I'd entered Skiboo one morning – and my heart missed a beat. He wasn't there. Or, rather, he wasn't in his usual place. There was a plastic cover on his heated cot, and all the wires and tubes were folded away. Luckily, the nurses saw me before I had time to think the worst. 'It's OK – he's over here in the incubator!'

At first, I took this as a sign that he was worse. But, actually, it was a mark of his progress. He now didn't need constant supervision, and could sleep happily in a safely enclosed environment where they could gradually reduce his dependence on oxygen. When he'd done well there for a few more days, he was allowed out into the air. Now he was in a conventional transparent hospital cot, still wired up to bleepers and monitors, but breathing ordinary air. And all the time, his respiration was becoming more normal. His little chest didn't cave in the way it had at birth.

But he was losing weight. Now he needed food. He was fast asleep. The midwife undid the end of his gastric tube, and injected his first feed down it. Then she held it up, and we watched the little dribble go down, and then inside him. What an extraordinary business, I thought. I watched in awe. Even more when, an hour later, the sister suctioned up, again through the gastric tube, the contents of his stomach to see if he'd digested that little drop of milk. He had – so Dr Rom decided he could have another in another hour's time.

'Let's not rush things,' he said, calmly. 'He's growing slowly but surely....' Let's not rush things, I agreed, seriously worried about whether I could manage any more milk.

Meanwhile, in a special fridge in the nursery next door, other women were refrigerating spare bottles of their produce. Pints and pints of the stuff, all carefully labelled – ready to provide overnight feeds for their bouncing babies. I felt totally inadequate. Thank goodness Supi wasn't expecting too much of me. Come to think of it, he hadn't even noticed he'd been fed at all. Soon, as with all healthy babies, he did need more – and luckily, I was able to provide it. I was proud that I could.

As I used to sit at his cotside, spending hours holding, changing and feeding my little baby amid all his wires and tubes, I watched the other players in this strange, gentle soap opera. I chatted to and listened to the other mums and dads, and all the support cast of relatives who passed through – some just for a few hours, others for weeks, like me. And for the first time in my own experience of motherhood, I learned that parenting can be about death, as well as life.

One morning, I walked in, full of the joys of spring, wheeling the breast pump before me, when a tragic sight met my eyes. A baby had come in the night before – and I'd seen him in his incubator before they pulled the screens around. He (it might have been a girl, I never knew) had been so white. That's what struck me hard. His little body was so very white. No colour at all. While I had quietly fed Supi, in the corner of the unit, several doctors had been talking in hushed voices over the little baby's incubator. The tone of their voices had been very serious and sad. That baby must have something terrible wrong with him, I thought – and didn't dare to ask anyone more.

Now, as I opened the Skiboo door, I heard a sound I'll never forget – the heartrending sound of a mother's pitiful wailing. I never saw her face. She sat with her back to the world, but I could see that she was holding her little white baby in her arms. She was rocking backwards and forwards, with her baby tight against her chest, her long, black hair draped down her back. Backwards and forwards, rocking, and wailing at the wall. Her baby was dead.

My eyes shot to my little Supi, sleeping in the corner. From the doorway, I could see his monitors bleeping and flashing as usual. A nurse came up to me: 'Can you come back in a few minutes?' she asked me, softly. I nodded, meekly, and went back to my room silently, suddenly aware of the savage, primitive cruelty of childbirth and motherhood. Until then, I had known only the joy. There, but for the grace of God, I thought...

Another incident sticks out in my memory, from those days in special care. It was the morning that we all heard on the news that Eric Clapton's son had died. He was called Conor – and he'd been with his mother, staying in a high-rise apartment block in New York. By some dreadful freak accident, a large window had been left open in their apartment. Conor, a typical little rascal of six, had been rushing around the room, and had fallen out. He fell fifty-three floors to his death.

It was in all the papers. The morning TV programmes were discussing it. The whole maternity wing of our hospital was subdued. Everyone seemed to be in a state of shock. Mothers held their new babies closer to their breasts. In corners, people were whispering: 'Isn't it dreadful? Did you hear? He was such a lovely-looking child....' And we were all asking the doctors: 'Surely he would have blacked out before...' No-one wanted to finish the sentence. All day, nurses, doctors and patients were shaking their heads in disbelief and sorrow. I vowed that we would put bars on our windows as soon as we got home.

I meant to write to Eric Clapton. Mike and I had known him when he was married to Patti. They were a smashing couple, mainly because they were so normal, despite their legendary status to anyone who'd lived through the Sixties. We had once, at a party, talked about our mutual liking for Gucci leather-ware, and I'd told Eric that Mike had bought me – as a birth-day gift – a briefcase from Milan. I joked that what I really wanted next was a vanity case to match. But that it could only be bought in Milan.

Several weeks later, and totally out of the blue, Patti rang me and said that Eric had just come back from touring in Milan, and had brought back a Gucci vanity case for me. I was stag-gered, because it had only been a chance remark. But he'd remembered, and even got the colour right.

Now, years later, I wanted to tell him that, though none of us had ever known his son, we all cared so very much. Conor's death had affected everyone in the hospital very deeply. I meant to write, but I never did – afraid that I might intrude upon his grief. I learned myself, later that same year, that such letters are very important. And that expressions of regret, or sympathy, never intrude. They really help.

I was ready to leave hospital well before Supi – so when the team from *TV Weekly* rang to see how I was, I told them I was fit to present the show. They sent the car to the hospital to collect me, and I left Mike at Supi's cotside in the Skiboo. When I reached the Southampton studios, I proudly showed off my Polaroid snaps of Supi. I missed him dreadfully – and it seemed strange, being made-up and dressed for live TV just four days after giving birth, but I knew Supi was doing well, and couldn't be in a safer place. The *TV Weekly* team – Chris, Peter, Roy, Tony and Jane – were all so supportive. Later that year, I was to learn the blessing of their friendship. Then the car returned me to hospital – where I got back to the breast pump.

One evening, Mike and I went out to dinner at a restaurant just around the corner. The nurses had promised to ring on our mobile phone if there was any emergency – but it was our first night out in a long time, and I longed to enjoy a comfortable meal again – one where I could bend in the middle, eat without heartburn, and have a glass of wine. At the rate of one millilitre every two hours, I couldn't see how a drop of wine would be harmful to the baby!

I had promised Supi I would be back later to feed him, and I'd reminded all the midwives, because I didn't want them to think I was away, and so feed him themselves. The sister made sure of that. When I came back, Supi was still fast asleep, next to his Wellington teddy. And, like a little parcel, he had a stick-it note on his back:

'18th March, '91. DEAR EVERYONE. MY MOTHER PHONED AT 2030HRS AND WILL BE IN FOR MY NINE PM FEED. SO PLEASE DON'T FEED ME, BUT KEEP ME HAPPY IF I WAKE. LOVE, SEBASTIAN.'

I took my camera out from the cupboard underneath his cot, and snapped a picture.

Shortly after that, Supi was allowed out of Skiboo and into the nursery for half an hour – so that he could be cuddled by his brothers and Alex, who'd been impatient to hold him. It became a family photo session, with everyone having the long-awaited chance for a hug and a pose. The boys sat in one of the large nursing chairs, and held him between them. They beamed with pride. What fun they were going to have together – what mates they would be. Oliver at three, Jamie, just two years old, and Supi, who was still three weeks short of his due date – but looking bigger and stronger every day.

The midwife who delivered him looked in. 'Quite a handful,' she laughed. 'It won't be long before they're all following you around like three little ducks!'

I was relieved that they were at last all together. My three boys.

A few days later, I agreed to do a short questionnaire for a regular feature in the *Daily Express*. They said it would only take two minutes, as they were set questions which they asked all the celebrities.

'What's your proudest achievement?' asked the girl reporter at the other end of the phone.

'Having three healthy sons,' I replied.

I don't know why the next question came next, but it did.

'And what's your greatest fear?'

'Losing them,' came the automatic response.

I couldn't have known how awfully ironic that simple comment was to be.

Chapter 6

He seemed so tiny when we brought him home – but he already had a great character. He seemed to know exactly what he wanted, but he wasn't a howler or a screamer – he just insisted, with a quiet determination which led us later to think that he would become the family diplomat. It's astonishing how little babies can very quickly impress you with the depth of their character. Supi would sit in the middle of the floor, in his baby bouncy chair, and run things. If his two brothers were arguing, he would gurgle or coo, immediately grab their attention, and so prick the bubble of tension.

Oliver had been awaiting, with some degree of understanding, the birth of his baby brother with impatience. He now revelled in his company, helping to feed and change him with excitement and curiosity: 'Why does his tummy button stick out?'

Jamie, on the other hand, was feeling a little displaced as baby of the family. He still had a bottle (of water) at night. But now he wanted to carry it around with him during the day, too. There was no doubt he was jealous – or at least anxious. But he only showed his worries to the adults, by wanting more cuddles, more loving. And, of course, he hated us holding the baby. Sometimes, while I was feeding Supi, happy that the other two were busy with Alex, or building something out of Duplo or Sticklebricks, I would catch Jamie out of the corner of my eye. He would be looking at me, with just a hint of resentment. He'll get over it with time, I thought. But he never showed any hostility towards Supi himself. As long as Supi wasn't actually in our arms, he was OK. In fact, Jamie became a dab hand at helping to feed him. He loved and understood bottles, after all. And, on car journeys, Jamie would help plug Supi's dummy in, if it fell out!

But two weeks home – and Supi caught a cold. With his prematurity, and his history of breathing problems, it was a difficulty he could have done without. But, I suppose, having two older brothers – both of whom played daily with other children at nursery school – it was hardly surprising that he succumbed to a virus. It was a tense time for me, though. I slept Supi in a Moses basket next to my bed. Now I tipped it up, so that he was almost sleeping uphill – and I steamed the room until the wallpaper came off the walls.

During the worst snuffly period, I stayed awake most of the night, holding him upright against a pillow. But as soon as he was a little better I propped him up on a cushion in his own basket, and under a makeshift tent made of sheets – to try and minimize the damage being done by the steam to the walls. Despite trying to watch him every moment, I dropped off to sleep myself. When I awoke, several hours later, Supi was sleeping happily inside the tent. But he'd slid down the tipped basket, and was in a quaint sitting position at the bottom, with his knees bent over the side, and his feet dangling in mid-air.

In the bedside cupboard above our heads was the apnoea alarm, packed away after our traumas with Jamie. Even in the worst of Supi's cold, I never once thought to get it out.

The cold almost over, I now needed some sleep, so we called in an old friend, the maternity nurse who had helped us with Jamie nearly two years before, Nanny Anne Robinson. Anne had a wonderful, soft and gentle way with babies. A very quiet person herself, she would rock and sing to them for hours on end. Supi loved her – and she stayed with us for several weeks.

With such a great deal of professional help – and both sets of grandparents happy to come round and lend a hand – we were determined that Supi should join in everything the others did. We travelled to the Lake District for a short holiday, we wheeled along the Mall to join the crowds watching the Trooping of the Colour, we had a day out at Thorpe Park, where the bigger boys delighted in petting the animals at the Farm. Everything they enjoyed, Supi did too. And, because my TV commitments were over – and Mike, being the managing director of his station, could schedule his time his own way – we kept ourselves very busy indeed. The boys were thirsty for new and exciting experiences.

But it was also time for a rethink domestically. I was no longer working – and didn't know whether *TV Weekly* would be recommissioned in the autumn. It was a difficult decision – but we began to realize that we no longer needed, nor could afford, a nanny. The two big boys were spending most mornings at nursery school. Soon, Oliver would be there all day. Looking after three little ones under four years of age would not be easy – it isn't for anyone – but I relished the prospect.

Alex understood completely – and promised she'd always stay in touch. She agreed that she'd start looking for another job. I didn't want her to go until she was totally happy with her next position.

You don't give away gold lightly.

Supi's health was generally fine, though we kept in touch with Dr Rom, especially throughout that first cold. Private doctors are expensive, however, and we decided that now we would make far more use of our National Health GP's practice, which was excellent, although always hellishly busy.

Our health visitor was one of the best. Her name was Anne, too. (At one point, we had three Annes in the house, all weighing Supi together!) She had helped us with Oliver and Jamie – and was delighted when she was called around to our home again. 'This house is always a happy place for children,' she said once, which made me very proud. We were a little worried because Supi had a touch of oral thrush inside his cheeks and

63

on his tongue – and he wasn't feeding (now on bottles – I hadn't been that successful at the breastfeeding!) with his usual enthusiasm. The doctor gave us the antibiotic Nystatin – a yellowish liquid which smelled of almonds and which tasted sweet and sticky. We had to squirt one dropper-full in his mouth four times a day. He hated it, but it cleared the infection very quickly.

He also had a slight problem with one testicle. It occurred to me slowly, over a few days, but soon I was sure that his left testicle was slightly swollen. I mentioned it to Anne, the health visitor, who agreed that it might need medical attention. Off to the doctor again. Yes, it was a hydrocele, a swelling usually caused by excess fluid. It wasn't painful, I was assured. And, indeed, Supi didn't seem concerned about it at all. It wasn't usually harmful in any way, the doctor continued. But she said she would refer Supi to a specialist. Did I want to go private, or NHS?

'Is it urgent?' I asked.

'No,' she replied. 'He's not in any pain, and it's not harmful in any way – so you don't need to see a specialist quickly....'

'In that case, let's go with the National Health Service.'

'Right,' she said. 'I'll make the arrangements, and you'll be notified about your appointment within the next few days, I should think.'

The letter came the following week, as we neared the end of May. It was for 15 August. I had a flicker of doubt. Where the children were concerned, I always liked to be on top of any health problems they might have, no matter how trivial. This would be the first time I would wait so long to get anything done. Still, if Supi was in no pain, and it wasn't dangerous... I decided to wait.

Our bedroom looked dreadful. I hadn't liked the wallpaper much anyway, but now it was curling up and dying. Corners were coming away where the steam from Supi's humidifier had strayed. And over my side of the bed, one piece was falling off.

We'd been wanting to redecorate, and redesign the room for ages. Now it was crying out for attention.

Supi's own bedroom was ready for him – I had prepared it while I was pregnant. It was covered in a Habitat wallpaper, a balloon pattern in bright primary colours. How did I find the time in those days? I had painted the wardrobe and cupboard knobs to look like balloons, and even given them tiny, dangly strings. I'd made big fabric balloons to hang in the top corner, to hide the damp patch on the ceiling, and the centrepiece was a hot-air balloon lampshade, which we'd bought in Australia. The big boys had used the room as an upstairs playroom while we were expecting Supi. Their toys were now shoved back under their beds, and Jamie's old cot brought out of the attic.

I'd also made cot bumpers, and a duvet cover, out of the balloon material. I'd bought a new mattress because I'd read something in the papers about cot death and old mattresses – and I didn't want to take a risk. I deliberately bought one made with cotton fabric on both sides, because the article had said there was something suspect about PVC. I went to John Lewis in Oxford Street, because ours was a particularly big cot and it wasn't easy to find the right size mattress in the ordinary high-street baby shops.

I bought new cot bedding, and a new sheepskin for Supi to lie on. I'd always been quite a fan of sheepskins for babies – since our first nanny, Debbie, had suggested we buy one for Oliver, to help him through his colicky nights. She said that they had used them at Great Ormond Street for babies who needed the extra feeling of security and comfort.

It was a trend which had started in New Zealand and Australia. Some say it was a cynical move by the sheepskin industry, to improve sales. But anyway, the belief grew that babies liked the feel of sheepskin, and thrived when sleeping on them. You couldn't go anywhere in Sydney without seeing a baby on one – in a pram or buggy. Even when the sun was at its hottest. Everyone said that as it was a natural skin, it breathed – so your baby couldn't get too hot. Toddlers still carried bits of sheep-skin with them, as comforters.

Supi seemed to like his. In fact, he loved his room. Whenever I carried him in there, his eyes would light up and he would smile. A little teddy bear mobile, made from coloured plastic like stained glass, dangled over his changing mat. There were white bars on the window, thanks to Eric Clapton's Conor, so we could safely have a breeze. The weather was getting warmer. We were going to have a good summer.

Alex was away on holiday. It gave me a taste of what life would be like as a full-time mother of three, without the help of a nanny.

The afternoons were the busiest. The trick was to get lunch down the big boys and their school tracksuits on while Supi was still asleep. Then there was the marathon task of making it past the front door. Our problem was that, living in central London, we were restricted to residents' parking spaces, which were few and far between. It was a miracle if you could ever park near the house. Then, if you did, you were loath to lose that space, but you had no choice if you had to do the school run. Keeping control over two little boys while trying also to hold a baby car seat, complete with baby, open car doors and negotiate the horrendous straps on two more car seats, and I was ready for a nervous breakdown. And that's before I'd even made it to school. Once I'd found an equally rare parking space outside St Mark's Nursery, the whole process would have to be reversed.

Then quickly home – because 2.30 was time for Sebastian's afternoon feed. That would take at least half an hour, plus a nappy change, and then it would be time to collect the boys again at 3.15pm.

Luckily, despite the fact that St Mark's was in the middle of trendy Camden Town, most of the other mums at the school gate were surprisingly normal – and usually looked as harassed as me. One notable exception was Catherine Bailey, wife of photographer David Bailey, who was there most days to collect Paloma and Fenton, their daughter and son. Even if she was in everyday clothes and no make-up, she looked as though she had just stepped off the Milan catwalk. He, by contrast, looked almost sinister, in a greyish-black duffle coat, and he always seemed to lurk in the shadows or behind trees until the school door opened. If you didn't know his famous face, you would probably think he was a spy or a secret agent! When we all turned up for school nativity plays and sports days, snapping away at our children with our Polaroids and Instamatics – he would be there, too, a doting dad like any other. But his snaps were probably infinitely superior.

If afternoons were hectic, then bedtime was mayhem. But now that Mike was busy redecorating the main bedroom, I would park Supi in his car seat, in the middle of the bare floor – and let him talk to his father while I bathed the big boys upstairs. He loved it, watching Mike move the ladder around the room, stripping wallpaper and chatting as he went. Often the radio or TV would be on, with a newsreader's piping voice in the background – and Supi seemed to enjoy the hive of activity. His eyes would bulge with enthusiasm and he would kick his socks off as he chortled.

By the time I had put the big boys to bed, with their musical box jingling out the mind-numbing dirge of Brahms's Lullaby, Mike and Supi had gone downstairs to the kitchen. I would come down the stairs to the bottom level and hear Mike chattering away to his youngest son as he applied all his culinary skills to a packet of Marks & Spencers fresh pasta, a pot of tomato and mascarpone sauce, and a green salad with hazelnut oil dressing. It was one of our favourite quickie dishes – and tasted as mouth-watering as if Mosimann had served it up himself. Now Supi, his car seat balanced carefully on the kitchen bench, would watch us as we ate, and gurgle along with the adult conversation.

He was so easy to love, such great company. And those little eyes at time seemed so wise. I had never seen Mike so relaxed with a baby. He loved all his children, I know. But he had always appeared to be one of those men who gets on best with them once they're older, can do things, and can hold meaningful conversations. Here, with Supi, he seemed to have found a mutual path of communication which belied the baby's age.

It seems so fanciful to describe it now – as if we might be accused of wishful thinking, or retrospective sentimentality. But I remember him saying, on one of those tomato and mascarpone evenings, as he nodded towards his miniature sous-chef in the bouncy chair: 'He is amazing, this one....'

I felt it, too. Not that we loved him any more than our other sons. I could never be one of those mothers who have a preference between her children. To me, that seems terribly cruel. Every child has a right to be loved individually, and loved completely. They may each be entirely different characters – but they all have endearing qualities, and it's your job as a parent to find them – and offer the love that will help them grow.

It's just that Supi felt different in a unique way. He drew you to him, like a warming light. He exuded happiness – and his laugh was infectious. Maybe it's because we had witnessed his fight for life during those days in the Skiboo. Maybe that's why his survival seemed so magical to us – and his existence so precious. It made him hard to put to bed at night. But such was his delight at the balloons in his room that I never felt guilty about leaving him there, even if he wasn't yet asleep. He had a favourite toy – a wind-up Babar musical merry-go-round. I would place it in the top corner of his cot. He would lie on his tummy, arms above his head, eyes wide, and watch the little elephants go round until he fell asleep. I would hear his breathing on the baby listener, and know that he was peaceful. And at three months, he slept right through the night, often for ten or eleven hours. No trouble at all.

Always, as prompt as the best alarm clock, he would wake at

ten to seven in the morning. Five ounces of warm milk, then a short break for a bath with mum, two more ounces, and then an hour's nap. That was his routine in the morning. I knew it well, and fitted my life around it. And while he slept, I would get the big boys up, and breakfasted.

Life as a family of five was beginning to take shape. Alex had found herself a new job, and was working with us for just a few more weeks. Right, we thought – time for a holiday.

We decided to go to Düsseldorf to visit Mike's old nanny. After the war, Mike's father – who was a soldier – had been stationed in Germany. One of the few perks for the family had been a German nanny. She was called Maria, and remained a dear family friend.

Mike drove over to Europe – and I and the children followed on by plane, with Mike's parents, who were going to stay with Maria. Maria and Mike had already met up, and they came to the airport to collect us. We left the Hollingsworths with Maria, and packed the children into the car for the drive down the autobahn to Strasbourg. We were going to stay for a few days with my younger sister and her husband.

Louise and Colin had met while they were both working at Marks & Spencers. Louise had been training as a personnel manager, and Colin as a manager. Just a year before, Colin had been offered the post of manager at the store in Strasbourg, France. They both saw it as a tremendous challenge – but it meant that my sister, whose own career was very important to her, would have to give up her job. She still missed working, but very much enjoyed the life in Strasbourg. And, indeed, it was a fascinating city – and the suburb where they lived, Mundolsheim, very pretty.

You could tell that, as a couple, they were beginning to think about having a family, too. Colin took expert charge of feeding Supi while the rest of us kept the bigger boys entertained, unpacked the car, settled ourselves in the spare bedrooms, and made tea. Louise and I stood quietly at the living-room doorway, secretly watching Colin cradling the baby.

'He's very good with him, isn't he?' I mused.

'Oh, yes...' agreed Louise. 'I think he'd really love children of his own.'

I suspect that, over the next few days, Supi revelled in his aunt and uncle trying out their child-rearing instincts. When I look back now at the video I made of that happy visit, Supi is always being held by one or the other of them. But my shots are so fast and furious. The pace of our life was quick, and my camera work as fleet. It seems I never held on to the shots for long enough. As soon as the camera has focused on Supi's little face, it's panning off again. I didn't seem to stay and savour the close-up. I didn't know how important it would be. Now it's so frustrating to watch that video. I find myself physically reaching out, to grab the image, to tell the TV to stop. I want to freeze-frame those moments, those fleeting seconds which were so short-lived, and sense them again.

It was time for a proper summer holiday. Where better to go than our old friend, Cyprus. Back to the land of Supi's conception!

Chapter 7

We were really enjoying our holiday in Cyprus. We thought we had everything – in particular three wonderful sons, less money or job worries than most people – and lots of love. That holiday revolved, as all good family holidays do, around the children's routine. Most of all, around Supi's because he was the smallest – now four months old. His feeds and naps dictated when the rest of us swam, ate and slept. I can see him now in a gloriously milky haze, either fast asleep in the shade while his big brothers played with Sticklebricks by the side of the pool or sitting up in his buggy, sunbonnet akimbo and a splodge of sunblock on his nose as he watched us eat meze in a seaside taverna.

But we did have just one business meeting to drive to – an hour up the Cyprus motorway to the capital, Nicosia. We'd be back in time for the afternoon swim. The children would hardly notice we'd gone. Alex would feed them, rock one to sleep with her foot while craftily assembling a Lego spaceship with her hands, nap them and have them changed into their swimming trunks by the time we'd returned.

But just a few minutes out of Limassol town, I was crying. When I'm in the car, the distance between me and my children is too great, and grows too fast. Mike calls it my 'blues', and wipes away the tears with comforting words and practical advice. Many fathers understand how it must feel – but they have never had the umbilical tie. Mothers don't lose it with the cutting of the cord.

I always think of my children when I'm in the car – especially if I'm being driven, and have time exclusively to think.

Ten minutes into the journey, and I'm often crying.... Always thoughts of them, at first happy, gradually becoming morbid. By the time I've reached the motorway, on my way into work – and especially if I pass the scene of a notorious crash or pile-up, the thoughts have become frightening – even more so if Mike is with me....

What if the children need us and we're miles away? What if we have a dreadful accident? Who would break the news to them? How would they cope? And I break my heart imagining them growing up without their parents. I want to be there for all that.... Many, many times I have nearly turned the car back, but never quite have. The sensible voice in my head tells me that all mothers think these thoughts – and that every parent must learn to let go.

Our appointment was with the owner of a firm which man-ufactures beautiful children's clothes. He was a typical Cypriot – he loved children and spoke proudly of his own. We inspected his designs and samples – we were hoping that we could start an 'Anne Diamond' range of children's outfits. Mmm. Oliver would look nice in that one, I thought. And Jamie will grow into this one. There was nothing quite right for Supi, though. I asked if I could have samples for my boys.

All the way back, I wished the miles away, aching to see the boys again – who, of course, had hardly missed us. They had new outfits to try on – except Supi who was happier anyway in just a T-shirt and a nappy. When he took his tea-time nap, I took the video camera out of its case and shot some relaxed scenes of us all drinking Coca-Cola and changing into warmer evening clothes. I fixed the mosquito net over Supi's pram, and we went for a slow walk, dodging the sprinklers which were watering the hotel's thirsty grounds.

We went to the Bunch of Grapes for Sunday lunch. High up on a mountainous ridge, overlooking the sea, is a village called Pissouri. You have to know it's there, but word of mouth is the most effective method of advertising on an island like Cyprus – and so Pissouri enjoyed a regular influx of visitors, and boasted two or three large tavernas.

The Bunch of Grapes was a particular favourite with the British forces families who were stationed nearby at the RAF base of Episcopi. It was built of stone, and so was very dark and cool inside, but its main delight was the walled courtyard, canopied with vines, which allowed a gentle, flecked light to dimple the diners below. Mike and I had come here since our first visit to Cyprus in 1980 – well before we knew that we would marry and have children.

It was also a favourite haunt of an old mate of ours, Gordon Honeycombe, the ITN newsreader, who had joined TV-am in the early days to add a much-needed air of authority. He had discovered Pissouri and the Bunch of Grapes years before – and had been so impressed that he'd written a novel about it, *The Edge of Heaven* (a perfect description of the place), about a young Cypriot boy and a British officer's wife. Practically everyone in the village had a signed copy. And most of the young men swore that they were in fact the passionate male lead.

Though the Bunch was now owned by a Dutchman, the manager was a Briton. Over the years we had come to know John quite well, and always looked forward to the annual opportunity to meet up with him again, and with his German partner, Roswitha. They were always surprised when they saw us – because for the last few years we had turned up each time with a new baby. Now they met little Supi, and toasted his health in Brandy Sours – the best on the island.

We sat at one of their larger tables, covered with the customary red and white gingham cloth, clamped down against the wind with tableclips and weighted down with baskets of bread, bowls of hummus and taramasalata and tzatziki dips with village bread – and we talked. Once the gossip was out of the way, the conversation turned again to news from the

73

Middle East. Being in the restaurant business, John and Roswitha were a focus for news and reports. They also had close friends in all the neighbouring countries. The hostages in Beirut were big news. Rumour and counter-rumour suggested that something was going to happen – and soon. We talked of John McCarthy, and Terry Waite. Were they still alive? Roswitha said she'd heard that McCarthy was alive, but that Terry Waite had died long ago.

And so the hours went by. The children began to tire of eating, flicking flies out of their drinks, and playing with their father's sunglasses. We decided to go back to the hotel, where they could have a swim. We said goodbye. We knew that we would probably not return this holiday. We were flying back to Britain soon. Back to Luton airport.

Roswitha kissed the children goodbye – and planted a peck on Supi's nose. We walked out through the archway, festooned with scarlet and mauve bougainvillea, and made for the car.

'Hold it!' called Alex, who was slightly ahead of the rest of us. 'Go back a bit, under the arch, and I'll take a picture of you....' And she took a quick snap. That's the only picture I have of the five of us together. And even though you cannot see Supi's face – I was holding him against my shoulder because he was getting tired and a bit crotchety – I treasure it. The next time we would get our cameras out would be for Oliver's birthday, which was in just a few days' time.

We flew back with Monarch – one of the nicest airlines I've ever travelled with – because they had it just right when it came to looking after families with small children. I've been on so many planes where the cabin staff boast that they have 'baby-changing kits' and they know how to warm up a bottle for you. What they mean is that they used to have one or two nappies, but cannot find them now. That one loo, down at the very farthest end of the cabin, has a baby changing table – but there's no room to breathe in it. And somebody must have taught them that babies like milk boiling hot.

But Monarch seemed to know their business. Maybe they did a bit of research with travelling mums and dads. And they found out that you need to feed your children before yourself, and without your own lap-table being piled high with food. That children like sausages, sandwiches, burgers and chips – otherwise they don't feel they're on holiday. And that mums need help with boisterous two-year-olds – not scathing looks and disapproving glances.

Luton airport turned out to be a much nicer place than Heathrow, too. It's funny how your perception changes once you've got little ones....

We had tons of washing when we came back – and we seemed to spend the next two days dealing with it. I went supermarket shopping for the birthday party. The invitations had gone out long ago – it was to be a teddy bears' picnic. I knew that our local Sainsbury's had most of the required goodies – teddy biscuits, chocolate teddies, even teddy crisps. We had teddy pastry cutters – and we could use them to cut sandwiches, too. I came home burdened with boxes of teddy plates, cups and jelly dishes, paper tablecloths, and teddy bunting. I'd checked out the party shop in Camden Lock. They had big foil teddy balloons which they would fill with helium on the day, and I would have to collect them in the Range Rover.

And I had friends who had hinted that they would be sending around something very special. They worked for a public relations firm and Oliver, Jamie and I had helped them launch a charity fund-raising event, sponsored by the toy firm Fisher Price. Oliver and I had visited the toy factory in Peterlee, Yorkshire. One of the PR team, a woman called Paddy, had confessed to me, in a quiet moment during our visit, that she, too, had had three children. But one, a boy, had died of cot death. At the time, I hadn't known quite what to say – and she'd apologized to me for mentioning it. She was afraid it would make me fearful.

Everything was set for a great birthday for Oliver. It was 11

July, and the weather was warm and sunny. Alex went out to buy a present which she knew Oliver would want. A big scooter, with large black tyres and alloy wheels which made it look a bit like a BMX bike. And she also bought a little red, smaller type – as an un-birthday present for Jamie.

We had to wait until the big boys were in bed that night, before trying to assemble the large scooter. Alex sat in the middle of the red carpet in the playroom, and tipped out all the bits, along with the nuts, bolts and Japanese instructions.

'Oh God!' she wailed. 'This doesn't make any sense!'

We laughed, as Mike offered to fetch his tool kit from the garden shed. I was feeding Supi his regular evening taste (it was never enough to be called a meal) of mashed banana. Then, as Alex appeared to be getting more successful, I sat on the red couch and gave Supi his evening bottle. He would usually polish off all eight ounces, and burp magnificently before bedtime.

'There!' announced Alex, triumphantly, a shiny black and chrome scooter in her hands. 'That's it. Now how can I wrap it up without it looking like a scooter?'

Supi stared at it – and started to coo contentedly. His eyes shone. He looked as thrilled as the rest of us. I bounced him gently on my knee. 'It's a scooter, Soops,' I whispered in his ear. 'Play your cards right, and you'll inherit that when you're older!'

And then I took him upstairs to bed. I remember that evening so well – because everything seemed perfect. When I carried him into his bedroom, he was snuggling into my shoulder – but I could sense his usual 'perking up' when he saw the balloons. It was quite warm, so I pulled down the top sash window about eight inches, to let in more fresh air. And then I laid Supi down, on his tummy, on the sheepskin. I wound up his Babar merry-go-round and watched him as he held his head up high and gurgled at the little revolving elephants.

He was wearing just a T-shirt (one we'd bought in Australia

with little koalas and hot air balloons) and a nappy. Should I put a shawl over him, I wondered? No, he was probably warm enough. Anyway, I would come and check on him again soon, and I could decide then.

So I said goodnight to him, and left the door ajar. He was accustomed to getting himself off to sleep, he never cried – he was what lots of mums would call a 'good baby'. At any rate, I knew he was happy in his own cot, and his own room.

I went into the other boys' room. They were sound asleep, too. Then I returned downstairs, where I switched on the baby listener. I heard the last strains of the merry-go-round jingle, and then could quite clearly hear Supi's gentle breathing.

I checked them all a couple more times that night, before Mike and I went to bed ourselves at about 11pm. I took the baby listener with me and plugged it in by my bedside, where I also had a bottle warmer, with which to warm Supi's morning feed.

I was adjusting the volume control on the listener. Downstairs among the bustle of the kitchen, it was turned up high. But in the bedroom, I needed to reduce the volume, so that Supi's movements could be heard without the hum of the receiver keeping us awake.

'He's breathing a bit heavily tonight,' Mike remarked. I listened more closely. Yes, he did sound a little more snorty than usual, but nothing alarming. Maybe he was brewing another cold.

Chapter 8

It was a lovely, warm, bright summer morning. I looked at my clock. Ten to seven. Supi would be waking soon. Mike had been downstairs making an early morning cup of tea. He handed mine to me, and also a cold bottle of baby's milk from the fridge. I popped it into the bottle warmer, and switched it on.

'It's a wonderful day,' I said, delighted that the weather should smile on our teddy bears' picnic. Discarded sandwiches and sausages on sticks might be acceptable when squashed into the lawn. In the carpet, they're a nightmare. I dreaded the thought of having to do the party indoors, as there were about thirty small children and as many adults. Maybe we'd be lucky.

'Don't be so sure,' warned Mike. 'It looks almost stormy. It could rain. I wonder if we should think about hiring a marquee? There's bound to be someone who'll hire one out at short notice....'

Ours was a London garden – I'd never thought of it as big enough to take a marquee.

'How small do they come?' I asked.

'No idea,' said Mike. 'I'll go outside and pace it out...Ollie up yet?'

We both pulled on our clothes and headed upstairs – straight for the big boys' bedroom, where I could hear them talking excitedly. Oliver beamed as we all burst in and sang 'Happy Birthday to You'.

'Your presents are downstairs,' I told him. 'So hurry up and get dressed....'

I went to check Supi. I was a bit surprised he hadn't woken yet. The bustle and banter behind me were all happiness as I opened the door to the balloon room. I could see Supi fast asleep in his cot, his left arm dangling out through the cot bars, his face away from me and the top of his head jammed against the cot side. He had wriggled his way off the sheepskin, towards the top left hand corner of the mattress. He often did nowadays. He was trying to crawl.

Maybe I'll leave him for a few more minutes, I thought. Then I can have a quick bath on my own. I'll just check he's OK....

I walked over to him and lightly touched the dangling arm. It was cold. But then, arms which dangle out of cots, over the sides of beds, or out from under duvets, are often a bit cold. I leaned forward and touched his other arm. It was cold, too. Ice cold. I lifted his little hand – and my heart stopped.

His whole body lifted up with it. His head, shoulders, chest – everything. He was stiff. Like a little marble statue of a baby lying in a bed. He was stone cold. I rested his hand back down on the sheet, and backed away, drawing breath as I stepped.

I could hear the other children coming into the room, behind me. I backed up to the doorway, and turned to Alex. 'The baby's dead!' I heard myself saying – and then, louder: 'The baby's dead!'

Alex stood, incredulous. The two little boys looked up at me. They didn't understand.

'Oh my God, the baby's dead,' I said again. And now I knew it must be true, because I heard myself quite distinctly saying it. I wailed : 'Where's Mike?'

'He's in the garden, I think...' Alex faltered, and then Oliver and Jamie let out piercing screams.

I ran back into Supi's room, to the window, which over-looked our back garden. I could see Mike below, pacing out the lawn for that marquee. I screamed his name, louder than I've ever screamed in my life, and pulled at the bars of the window. One bar came clean away in my hand. I rapped furiously on the window-pane – and I saw him look up, his face at first curious, changing within a split second to horror. I saw him start to run.

I turned back to the cot. I'd never seen a dead person before. But I knew death – I'd seen dead pets, long ago, in my childhood. I recognized the hopeless, despairing, numbing certainty of rigor mortis – now terribly reproduced here in my own precious son. I picked him up, and held him to my chest. The cold of his body was chilling – the back of his head, where I always put a steadying hand, felt like a ball of stone, but with a sad little dent in it, where he'd pushed it against the cot bars. I leaned his body back slightly in my arms, so that I could look at his face. It was cruelly squashed, where his face had rested on his cheek. And it was white, dead white, except for purple blotches, where the blood had gathered.

My Supi, my little boy. I hugged him tighter. My little Supi, dead....I sank into the white wicker nursery chair by the bottom of the cot. I couldn't believe it, and I felt somehow removed from reality. It felt as though I was in a film. It's at moments like this in movies, or in books, that the character faints or collapses in shock. But it doesn't happen like that in real life. You just go on, reeling at the gathering pain and growing realization.

I heard Mike bound up the stairs. Outside, on the landing, I heard a breathless: 'What's happened?' and Alex replying, still in shock, 'The baby's dead.' And the boys still screaming, whimpering and sobbing.

Mike ran in, panting. I looked up at him. I was still holding Supi close, but his little arms, so stiff, did not return my embrace. Mike later said that the sight which met his eyes, of me absurdly rocking this little statue, with those arms sticking out on each side, is one he'll never forget.

'He's dead,' I cried. 'Oh, Mike, he's dead....' And then the tears came, in final recognition of the truth.

Mike's face still registered shock. 'Can we...? Is there nothing we can do...?'

'No,' I wailed. 'He's dead, Mike...he's been dead for a long time.'

I don't know how long we just clung to each other, with our dead child between us, before Mike said he must call the police. I heard him tell Alex to take Oliver and Jamie downstairs, and try to give them breakfast. I just clasped Supi tighter – and the cold was burning into my chest. I stroked the fine down on his head – he was losing his new-born dark hair and growing into a blond – but the head beneath it was frigid, although the flesh still soft.

And the feeling of being in a film continued. Everything went into slow motion – things happened around me in a blurry haze. And I could almost see myself and my child, confused and helpless. Mike appeared again and again, constantly checking on me whilst trying to organize the boys, Alex, and call the police, the doctor, and my friend Shirley.

He hadn't spoken to Shirley for about two years. Long ago, they had got along extremely well, but after a terrible argument Mike had decided he didn't want anything to do with her. It had been very painful for me, since she and I were so close. So we met away from Mike, and often during the day when he was at work. Now, on this dreadful morning, one of his first instincts was to call her. But he didn't know her phone number – and the only one he had in his Filofax was out of date. So was the number in our family phone book. Mike was distraught – he knew he must find her. I think he was afraid that I might go to pieces.

He phoned the police, who said an officer would be around straight away. And then he phoned Peter, our private GP, who had become a friend. His wife, Gilly, answered the phone. Peter had already set off for the practice. But, ever the professional doctor's wife, she wasted no time on tears and sympathy. 'I'll get him to call you straight away,' she promised. And within two minutes, he was ringing from his car.

It was a call Peter must have dreaded returning. He had been so badly affected by the cot death which had happened to him just two years before. Being a loving father of four children himself, he had told me once that he could imagine nothing worse than cot death.

'You know there's nothing I can do,' he warned Mike.

'Yes, but please – come for Anne's sake...' Mike pleaded with him.

And then, just as Mike put the phone down, it rang again. It was Shirley, slightly nonplussed to have got Mike, and a bit embarrassed. 'Oh, er...hello, Mike,' she stammered. 'Can I speak to Anne, please? I just wanted to wish Oliver a happy birthday....'

Nothing could have prepared her for Mike's distressed response. 'Shirley, Shirley – thank God you've rung! Please come, please come round. Shirley, our baby's dead!' She blurted out the only remark that was needed: 'Mike, I'll be there in half an hour!' She had a taxi waiting outside her front door. She had been going to a meeting, and wanted to speak to Oliver before she left – but now she was on her way to help us. And we needed her.

The doorbell rang. It was a policeman. He asked to go straight upstairs. Mike brought him into Supi's bedroom. I was still sitting in the little white chair, cradling our baby. The young policeman stood in the doorway for a second, taking in the scene. Then he removed his helmet, and I could see that his eyes were brimming with tears. He held out a hand to me.

'I'm so sorry,' he started – and then took his hand back, to wipe a tear from his cheek. 'I'm so terribly sorry. You see, the same thing happened to me, too....' And then tears overcame him.

This time, I held out a comforting hand to him. I didn't know what to say, and nor did he. His name was Ken Wake and fate had cruelly sent him to attend to us, not long after he had endured the agony of his own child's cot death. Mike stood back, almost unable to take this all in, and then he put an arm around the policeman's shoulders.

Later, when he had gone back downstairs, Shirley came in, hesitant at first, and then rushing to me with her arms outstretched.

I had put Supi back in his cot. I longed to lie him on his back, so that I could see him in a more natural position. But it only emphasized his terrible stiffness. And I couldn't bear his little squashed face – it was just too awful to look at. So I put him back down in the only way I could – in the same position in which he had died.

Our doctor, Peter Wheeler, came. He stood quietly at one side of the room, leaning awkwardly against the changing table. He muttered something again about babies forgetting to breathe – and asked if I wanted sleeping pills. I said no. I felt a strange mixture of pity for him, and impatience at his helplessness. For the first time I realized that doctors were not the gods I'd always assumed them to be. They do not always have the answers. And, faced with a situation for which they're untrained – death – they are as ineffective as the next person.

Mike's sister, Sue, came to sit with me. We both sat on the floor near the cot. I was stroking Supi's hand. I wanted so badly to hold him – but it was such awful agony when I did.

'I know it seems stupid,' I confided in Sue, 'but I want to put socks on him – his feet look so cold.' His feet and hands were purple. It looked ghastly on such a helpless little baby. My instinct was so strongly telling me to wrap him up, and make him warm.

'It's not stupid,' said Sue. 'If you want to put his socks on, then do.'

I went to the drawer where I kept his tiny, beautiful clothes. Together Sue and I silently pulled the little white socks on to his feet. Still, he looked so cold. So I took a white shawl – the one I'd wrapped him in when he left Skiboo – and draped it around his body. Now he looked comfortable and warm. Sue and I sat back on the floor – and just cried.

There was another knock on the bedroom door. Mike came in and introduced another policeman, a plain clothes detective inspector. He was kindly, offered his sympathy, and looked around the room. 'Was it this warm in here overnight?' he asked.

I suppose it was quite warm. The sun was shining, though not directly into the room, since it was south-facing, and didn't get direct sunlight until afternoon.

'The window has been open all night,' I murmured. Only later did I think that he must have seen Supi, now wrapped up in a shawl, and may have assumed that he had been dressed like that all night, too. I could clear up any confusions later, when I presumed I would be asked lots of questions.

Mike came back to me, and persuaded me to leave Supi for a short while and come downstairs. I grabbed his arm: 'Could we...? Is it possible...? Could we donate any of Supi's organs?'

It was something I'd always felt strongly about. Now I remembered an interview which Esther Rantzen had done on *That's Life*, with a woman who had lost her son in an accident. He was about ten years old, and he'd fallen off a wall. Just a distance of about eight feet – but he had been killed. She said the decision to donate all his useful organs had helped her through her grief – since she felt that part of him had lived on, had benefited other children. And it helped make some meaning of his death. Now I wondered if, somehow, Supi could help other little babies like him. Maybe he could help a blind child to see. Or his little heart could save another baby's life. I thought of our tense days in special care – and how I would have wanted such help, if we'd been told that only a transplant could save Supi's life.

I was worried that my suggestion might offend Mike – but he was pleased I'd broached the subject. 'I'll ask...' and he went off to find the policemen. Minutes later, he came back,

85

shaking his head. 'It's too late for his organs to be used – and anyway, they won't allow you to donate if there has to be a post-mortem. And they are going to have to do one, I'm afraid.'

I would have loved Supi to have had the chance to help another baby. Now, as well as having his life snatched away from him, he was to be denied that, too. It seemed even more cruel.

I wanted a bath. Still with the feeling of being in a movie, somehow distanced from reality, I went to the main bedroom, and had a bath and washed my hair. Shirley stayed with me, her face a tortured blend of her own grief, and concern for me. It was only when I found myself drying my hair with the hair-drier, that I suddenly felt revolted by myself, doing something so trivial and selfish when my baby had just died. I turned to my friend: 'Oh, Shirley... My baby is dead, and here I am dry-ing my hair!'

I dropped the hairdrier down on the bed where I was sitting. It was such a small, insignificant act. Yet I was shocked that I could be doing it. But it was the first awful realization that life was to go on. It seemed like a hideous insult to the sad little body in the cot upstairs.

After my bath, and when I'd changed into clean clothes, I went on downstairs to the kitchen. I noticed it the second I entered the room. The large, yellow plastic Milton sterilizer, which dominated the sink area, had gone. One of Alex's first jobs in the morning was to do the baby's bottles. She had asked Mike what she should do now – and they had agreed to put all the bottles and baby-feeding paraphernalia away. They thought the sight of it all would just upset everyone. It hurt me that it had so quickly vanished. There was a gathering crowd of relatives and friends already, making gallons of tea. I accepted a cup, and reeled at my ability to drink.

Sandra, Alex's friend, who had helped out on the day of Supi's birth, had come round. Mike had met her at the front door, and she'd fallen into his arms, saying: 'Oh, Mike – it's every mother's nightmare....' Sue was still there, Shirley, and two policemen. Soon we were joined by Mike's parents. And Mike told me that he'd phoned my parents in Bournemouth, and my mother was already on her way, on a train.

Now Mike, his face lined and strained with concentration, set to work on the phone. He had made a list of those who needed to hear the news from us first, rather than on the TV or radio. The policeman had warned that there was a reporter outside the door already, and there would be more. That reporter, a girl from the *Daily Star*, had got Mike. She asked if what she'd heard was true. Mike said yes. And then she asked the classic: 'How do you feel?' He just looked at her, and quietly and calmly shut the door. From that moment onwards, neither of us went to the door again.

My agent, and our friend, Jon Roseman, arrived to help. He said the news had been on the radio bulletins as he'd driven up from his home in Sussex. He added that there was now a large crowd of some twenty reporters and photographers in the street outside. He turned on the TV in the living-room, and switched to *Sky News*. I watched in disbelief and horror as I saw shots of Mike and me laughing and chatting at some celebrity event, and heard the newsreader's voice-over about a baby being found dead.

I wanted to go back upstairs to Supi. Mike came with me, and we took Oliver and Jamie with us. I sat down on the floor again, and the two boys stood, curious but silent.

'Supi is dead,' I said to them gently, and they nodded, meekly. But I knew neither of them really understood what 'dead' was. I needed to make them understand that Supi had not disappeared in the night. I didn't want their last awareness of him to be my screaming and panicking.

'Look.' I motioned them gently towards the cot. They could see their baby brother inside, his head turned away to the wall, his left arm extended, a shawl covering him. 'You can touch his hand. See? It's cold, very cold...and that's because there is no life in him any more.'

Oliver felt Supi's hand, and then Jamie followed. They both looked serious, but calm.

'And see, if you put your hand on his back, you'll feel that he's not breathing....'

They both patted him lovingly on the back. Such a lot to take in. Such complexity to absorb when you're only two and four.

'That's what happens when you're dead. You don't breathe any more, and your body goes cold. And there's no life anymore. Supi won't be with us ever again.'

Then I grasped at something I knew both of them had heard of, since we'd talked about it so much over Christmas. 'He is going to Heaven, and he'll be with baby Jesus.'

Oliver looked from the cot, up to Mike and me. 'Why are you crying?' he asked, softly.

My eyes started watering again, and I was suddenly aware of how sore they felt. 'Because it's sad, Oliver. It's so very, very sad. We love him so much, don't we?' And they both nodded. 'We love him so much. And Mummy and Daddy are sad that he cannot stay with us any more.'

I asked them if they wanted to say goodbye to him, and they both said yes. Oliver went back to where his baby brother lay motionless in the cot. He stroked Supi's hand again. 'Goodbye, Supi,' he said, almost in a whisper, as though he wanted to keep that moment private.

Jamie copied him. His touch seemed, like the toddler he was, rather more robust. I could see the white flesh of Supi's hand dimple as Jamie pressed it. 'Goodbye, Supi,' he chirruped.

I was sure that, one day, they would be glad they had said a proper farewell.

Chapter 9

'Do you want a priest?' Mike asked me.

It jolted me out of the feeling of suspended animation which was almost cushioning me from the harsh facts. But, yes, I knew that I would like someone to come and give Supi the Last Rites. We agreed that I should ring the local Catholic Church. I was brought up a Catholic – and one of the traditions which stayed with me still, and often provided great comfort in times of need, was the lighting of candles.

There was the most beautiful and bustling Catholic church in the next street. Coincidentally, its entrance was opposite the back door to our local Marks & Spencers.

Whenever I went shopping, the children and I would pop into the church on the way – and light a candle. They loved the place, its peace, and the gentle faces of the saints in the statues. Whenever we had lost something, and needed to find it, we would light a candle to St Anthony. He always came up trumps. But since Christmas, and the stories of the Nativity at school, the boys had particularly come to like the statue of the Madonna and Child. They always lit several candles to her, using all my small change to buy them.

I had never met the priest – but I knew from the church, and the way it was always busy that he must be one of the more enlightened of the Catholic flock. After all, it was an inner city church, with a large Irish and Portuguese community – and the Church often sent their best young priests to such postings.

I sat down at the dining table, with the plain-clothes DI at my side, and prepared myself to make the call. I rang the number. A brisk voice answered: 'Yes, can I help?'

'I wonder if someone can come,' I stammered. 'I live just up the road, and I come into your church quite often. You see, my baby has just died...and I wondered if...'

'What's that?' said the voice. 'You say your baby has died? Well, I'm sorry, both our priests are out.'

'Ohh,' I quavered. 'When will they be back?'

'Well, not for a while...' said the voice. 'What did you want them to do?'

'Well, I just hoped that they could come round,' I ventured. 'And maybe say the Last Rites, or something...'

'Oh, no!' said the voice, 'you can only perform the Last Rites if someone is still alive – not if they're already dead...I'll just go and ask the old priest, he's upstairs. Hold on a minute....'

The DI turned to me and asked what was going on. I relayed to him what I'd just been told. He rolled his eyes skywards, impatiently.

The voice came back, after just a few minutes. 'I've spoken to the Father upstairs,' he said. 'He says you can only perform the Last Rites if it is still alive. There's nothing we can do if it is already dead...'

From being stunned, I was catapulted into outrage. 'My baby is not an it,' I blurted into the receiver. 'He's a he!' I burst into tears, and slammed the phone down.

The DI was absolutely incensed. He banged his fist on the table. 'That just about confirms everything I've ever felt about the Church!' he spat, then put a comforting arm around my shoulders.

Once I'd calmed down, Mike suggested we have one more try for a priest. The only other church with which we had any ties was St Mark's, where Oliver and Jamie went to nursery school. Mike rang Sheema, the nursery school headmistress, to ask for the vicar's phone number. She was so shocked at the news that she couldn't hold a practical conversation. We found the vicarage number in the phone book, instead, but all we got was an answering machine. I was exasperated, although many people might consider that I had no right to be. We had never actively supported any church. Why should we deserve their help now?

'Let's not bother any more,' I said, resigning myself to the belief that the Church was really only interested in its own.

One of Shirley's best friends was a priest. He was called Peter, and we'd both known him from our teenage years, when he'd been the new curate in our home town of Malvern. Now he was the chaplain at Harrow School. We both knew he was abroad at the moment.

'But he has a friend who might help,' said Shirley, thoughtfully.

'No, don't, Shirley,' I said. 'I really don't want someone we don't know....'

I looked around, at the room full of anxious faces. It struck me that we all looked so desolate. It was one of those times when, even if you spend most of your life ignoring the Church and its doctrines, you desperately need the sort of guidance and spiritual comfort only ritual can give.

'Please...' entreated Shirley. 'I've got an idea. Let me have one last try.'

With that, she disappeared downstairs to the privacy of the kitchen phone. Five minutes later, she emerged, looking slightly more pleased. 'The other chaplain is coming,' she said. 'You will really like him, he's lovely. And he wanted to come! Harrow is only just up the road. He'll be here in about half an hour.'

We had never met James, but no sooner had he been told the news than he offered to jump in his car. In fact, he had left home in such a hurry that he'd forgotten the white bit of his dog collar. He only remembered it when he was parking the car outside our house. As he reversed into a space, he caught sight of himself in the rear-view mirror. Since he was going to have to run the gauntlet of Fleet Street massed outside our front door, he thought he should look right. So he tore off a scrap of paper from his *A-Z* road map, and fitted it into his collar. No-one would ever have suspected.

If there is a Heaven, if there is a God, then James was sent to us that morning on direct orders. He was everything we needed, and more. He strode in quietly – and if he felt awkward or distressed by his task that morning, he never showed it. Mike and I took him upstairs and showed our little boy to him, as proudly as you would show off a newborn baby to a visitor.

'We've been told that you can't do the Last Rites if he's dead,' I said to James.

'Strictly that's true,' he answered, softly. 'But I can say prayers. We could have a little service here, around his cot. Would you like that?'

We nodded, and all three of us gazed quietly down on the little sleeping figure.

'He's not there any more, is he?' I said to James. 'That's just his body. What was Supi has gone, hasn't it? I've never been so sure of anything. He's just not there any more....'

Mike and I had both thought it, earlier that morning, when we had held him so tightly between us.

'No,' sighed James. 'He's not there any more. But this was his body, in which he lived, and so it is still very, very special.'

My mother still hadn't arrived – and Mike was told that the coroner wanted to take Supi's body soon. In the back of my mind, I knew that they must take him away – so that they could start their investigation into why he had died. I knew that was important. So, reluctantly, I accepted that we would have to go ahead with James's service without my Mum. I knew she would have wanted to be there, but we could not wait any longer.

Everyone came up to his little room. Mike and the boys, Shirley, Alex, Nana and Grandad Hollingsworth, Mike's sister Sue – and we stood in a semicircle around the cot. Supi, still apparently sleeping peacefully and unaware of the fuss going on around him, became the focus of our heavy eyes. At the end, we all said the Lord's Prayer together. Then they all left Mike and me alone with him.

'He's not here, is he?' I said again to Mike. We both leaned over the side of the cot, looking down at Supi's body, and stroked the shawl on his back. The tears were running down Mike's cheeks, as he agreed.

I looked up at the window. It was still magnificently summery outside, and the sun was beginning to come around to shine directly in on us. It must be nearly midday. I looked again at the top sash, which was still open about eight inches, as I'd put it the night before.

'Then where has he gone?' I asked. 'Where is he? He couldn't just disappear... He had such life, such a spark. That can't just evaporate, can it? It must be somewhere...'

'I don't know,' Mike sobbed. He put his arms around me, and we clung tightly to each other.

Finally, he wiped his own, and then my eyes. 'Come on. They want to take his body away. You don't want to see them taking him, do you? Come downstairs and sit in the bedroom for a bit.'

We both braced ourselves to say a last goodbye to our little boy.

I leaned over and kissed his upmost cheek.

I heard him breathe...Oh, my God! I heard him breathe!

'Mike...' I gasped. '*I heard him breathe....*'

But even as I said it, I knew I was deluding myself.

'Oh, God, Mike...' I wailed. 'I thought I heard him breathe... I thought I heard him breathe.' I wanted to collapse. I wanted to die. I wanted my baby back. *I wanted my baby back*. My arms felt so empty. Where had he gone? We had been robbed of our child just as cruelly as if someone had stolen into our house in the middle of the night and murdered him.

I sat in our bedroom, shaking in disbelief, and I heard the

steps of the people from the coroner's office go up to Supi's room and then down again. I heard the front door close behind them. They had taken him to the mortuary. I lay back on the pillow, and there, by my bedside, was Supi's morning feed, still standing in the bottle warmer. It was beginning to curdle.

Mike came in. 'They took him away in a really nice little carry-cot,' he said. 'I thought you'd like to know.'

I hadn't even thought about how they would carry him away. Mike had obviously been dreading the sight of a body bag.

The second policeman, the DI, had brought a leaflet with him from the police station. It was a photocopy of a factsheet published by the Foundation for the Study of Infant Death, and it had two holes punched in it, where it had, presumably, been in a file. Now it lay on the ottoman, in the centre of the living-room. Everyone had read it. It had given them something to do – there was a dreadful feeling of being in suspended animation, and of being besieged. Now I picked it up, and read it.

'Information for Parents following the unexpected death of their baby' it read, and I drank in the matter-of-fact, sensible words. That leaflet became our bible for the next few days. Its advice, on everything from how to arrange your own funeral service, to how to deal with children's questions, became invaluable as we coped with one of the worst tragedies any parent has to face.

My mother arrived. We fell into each other's arms. I could feel the double burden of grief in her embrace. She was breaking her heart for Supi, but also for me. And she looked so terribly betrayed by what had happened. She said afterwards that you simply don't expect your grandchildren to die before you.

Jon Roseman said we should agree a statement for the press. More reporters were clamouring outside, and needed some sort of quote from us. We put together a simple confirmation of the facts. Just as Jon was about to go to the door and deliver it, I stopped him. 'I think we should put the word "beloved" in there,' I added. 'I want them to know that he was loved.'

So the statement read 'their beloved son, Sebastian...' It seemed better but so terribly final. To me, it was a gravestone word.

I turned back into the room. Oliver was wearing the policeman, Ken Wake's, helmet. He and Jamie had melted into the background so tactfully all morning. They had been quiet and watchful – and the adults around them, particularly the policemen and James, the priest, had been delving in the Lego box with them. Now Oliver's face turned up to mine, and he said, not impatiently, but quite firmly, 'Mummy, can I open my birthday presents now?'

Yes. I had forgotten. It was Oliver's birthday. He was four years old.

We hurriedly made a few sandwiches. Shirley dodged through the reporters to buy a birthday cake from Marks & Spencers, and we huddled around the ottoman to light the candles. We sang Happy Birthday, and Oliver blew out the candles with as much delight as if the day had turned out the way it had been planned. We even took pictures with the camera I'd loaded especially for scenes of children, balloons and party games. Now I look back, I cannot think how we even smiled, let alone sang and posed for pictures. But we were in a haze of disbelief.

Later Oliver put on his helmet and knee-pads – all matching presents – and went to Regent's Park with Alex, to try out her gift to him. It was the scooter, the gift I had promised Supi that he would one day inherit.

I turned to James, who saw my despair. 'Don't ask me, because I don't know why, either,' he said, anticipating my question. 'God sometimes does awfully cruel things. I don't know why he should take the life of a little baby like Supi. I am angry, too.'

We were sitting quietly in the garden. I see-sawed between

phases of crying until there were no more tears left, and periods of total immobility. Suddenly, Jon Roseman appeared, and gently but firmly put his arms around James and me, escorting us inside. 'Don't look around,' he said. 'But there's a very large, long lens trained upon you both from a building over there.'

A particularly intrepid photographer had clambered upon the roof of an overlooking building. He had the sort of lens on his camera which I'd seen at polo matches, trained upon a distant Princess Di. We shut the French windows, and drew the net curtains across, and wept in private. The warm July sun, which should have been the icing on the cake of a jolly birthday celebration, was beating instead on an empty garden.

At about five o'clock it was clearly the end of the journalists' day. The reporters left. Already, our little boy's death was yesterday's news. But we were only just beginning to live it.

Chapter 10

It felt so strange that night driving with only two child seats in the back of the car. I couldn't get over the feeling that I was abandoning my baby, leaving him behind with total strangers. I had to keep shaking off the vision of his little body on a cold slab – or the nightmarish thought of a knife cutting into him.

But on another level of my mind was the nagging need to know what had happened to him. Why had he died? Was it a 'cot death', as the TV bulletins had already decided? Or had I done something stupid – something which I hadn't realized – to cause his death? Had I missed some vital sign of illness, or disease? Had I failed to hear him choking, perhaps?

It must be my fault, I was sure of that. Babies don't die unless someone does something wicked or negligent to them. I worried all the way down the motorway to Bournemouth, where we were going to stay with my parents, as Mike drove and the boys dozed, one gnawing his muslin comforter and the other sucking his bottle.

'Oh, no...' Mike groaned, as his eyes darted between the road ahead and the rear-view mirror. We were near our destination. 'I think we're being followed....'

It was nearly midnight. A pair of headlights was pursuing us, wherever we went. Mike took a few odd turns. The headlights persisted. We were only streets away from my parents' home.

'We don't want to lead him there,' said Mike. 'Or we'll never get a moment's peace. Can't they just leave us alone? Today of all days, couldn't they just leave us alone?'

Mike stopped the car. The other one overtook us, and

motored on ahead. Maybe we were wrong. Maybe they hadn't been following us. At any rate, they'd gone now. We turned down the road to my Mum's house. There, outside my parents' driveway, was our pursuer.

'So he already knows where we're going,' sighed Mike again. He turned the car around.

'Where are we going?' chorused the children, dismayed.

'I don't know,' answered Mike, angrily. I could see that he had been strong for long enough. He was near to breaking now, weighed down with the exhaustion of the long drive, on top of the shock, grief and disbelief which was oppressing us all.

We rang my parents from the car. My mother had returned earlier by train so that she could prepare rooms. 'We can't come,' I wailed at her. 'There's a reporter parked outside your door. They'll never let us alone. They'll be crawling in through the windows.'

My mother was alarmed. She could hear that both of us were panicking. 'Where are you going to go?' she asked.

'I don't know,' I cried. 'I don't know. Anywhere. We'll find somewhere.'

My elder sister, Sue (both Mike and I have sisters called Sue) was there too, waiting for us. She grabbed the phone. She could see that someone had to take charge. They were worried about our state of mind.

'Look, you've got to come here,' she said, almost angry with us. 'Think of those two little boys. They need to be put to bed. You need to rest. You need to be with people who love you. *You come on in, now...*'

By now, I was sobbing again. The children were wailing. Mike was agonized and exhausted at the wheel. Our pursuer had clearly decided not to sit it out – he had disappeared. When we reached the front door, we almost fell in. Sue grabbed us both, with a powerful grip, and steered us towards the sitting-room. My parents scooped up the children, their toys and clothes – and we all sank into the sofas, hurt and weary. Then, as Sue poured tots of whisky, we talked into the night, my father shaking his head in sorrow and disbelief. My mother put the children to bed – and Mike and I, now almost in a dream, went in their room to kiss them goodnight.

'Mummy,' called Oliver, as the lights went out. 'Mummy...?'

'Yes?'

'Mummy...?'

'Yes, Oliver?'

'Mummy... Why... Why, when a baby dies...?'

'Ye-e-e-s?'

'Why, when a baby dies... do you phone everybody?'

Mike and I didn't exactly go to bed at all – we lay on it, hugging each other and alternating between dozing and weeping. It was the longest night – and, as dawn broke to a cold, cloudy morning, we felt raw and frail. It was our first day without Supi – we had already made it to Day One, and our sheer survival felt like a betrayal of the little boy we loved. Oliver and Jamie were still asleep. I hadn't even thought to be afraid for them. Though the news bulletins had mentioned 'cot death' in their reports, I hadn't properly grasped the concept.

I sat in the dining-room with my mother, drinking tea, and staring out of the window at the drizzling rain outside. Mike said he was going out.

'Don't worry if I'm gone for a while, I just want to walk,' he said.

I sat like a zombie at my mother's dining table, and as I poured my second mug of tea, I realized that life was going on – even though I didn't want it to. Every sip felt like a disloyalty to Supi. As his mother, how could I go on living without him? How could I nourish myself, knowing that he was dead? How could I attend to the stupid trivia of life, like getting dressed, or eating food, when he had gone? The toast cloyed in my mouth, yet I still ate it. I went back to the bedroom, washed and dressed – and then got the children up, too.

They were overtired and anxious. But Oliver had new toys – especially the scooter – and Jamie had un-birthday presents to play with. Sue had suggested they spend the day at her house, with her husband, Dave, and her two sons. Adam and Stuart were teenagers, and absolute heroes to mine.

The morning newspapers clattered through the letterbox. My parents always had the *Daily Telegraph* and the *Daily Mail* delivered. Dad picked them off the floor. I don't think any of us were prepared for the shock of those front pages – particularly the size of the tabloid headline. 'ANNE DIAMOND BABY TRAGEDY,' it screamed.

'They say it was cot death,' read Dad. 'But how could they know? How could they possibly know?'

'What is cot death?' asked Mum. 'We didn't have it in my day... or at least I never heard of it. Why do they talk about it so much nowadays?'

The doorbell rang. I watched as my mother opened it. There on the doorstep, his clothes soaked through, with water cascading down his face, was Mike. He was totally drained of colour. He looked like a ghost. He must have been walking in the rain for three hours.

'I'm sorry,' he said quietly, when he had changed. 'I went down to the little church where your sister got married, and I just sat in the graveyard. It's easier in the rain – people can't see that you're crying...'

All Saints' Church, West Parley, is a tiny but beautiful medieval village church, set in glorious countryside, near a river with ducks and swans. It is so old that it still has box pews which had once been owned by local wealthy families. Though we were a family of lapsed Catholics, my mother sometimes went to services there and my sister, Louise, had chosen All Saints' for her wedding. One of the reasons was undoubtedly because of its picturesque quality. But another was because its vicar, Fred Rason, was such a lovely man. He was a former businessman who had received a 'calling' and he was refreshingly open-minded about ministering for anyone, not just regular worshippers.

The following morning, a Sunday, Mike and I left the children with my parents, and drove down to All Saints', just to sit quietly inside. We thought we might stay for the morning service. When we got there, the door was open. We read on the noticeboard that the service would be in half an hour – so we sat in the pews for a while, holding hands and thinking. Then we walked in the grounds.

People were beginning to arrive. There were a lot of Sunday best suits, and plenty of large hats. As we made our way towards the main entrance I was aware that we had been recognized by several ladies, who were talking worriedly. One came over, and held my arm. 'I'm so sorry,' she said. 'About what happened to your baby. It's simply dreadful... I shall say a prayer for you today.'

And then another woman beckoned us to one side. 'Are you sure you want to go in?' she asked, her face concerned. 'Did you know that this morning's service is a baptism? Maybe you shouldn't...'

Suddenly I was aware that there were a lot of little babies going into the church, held proudly in their parents' arms. So that was why there were so many posh hats. The woman was right to warn us. We did not belong there that morning. We turned and walked away, through the procession of churchgoers, and up the path to where we had parked. At the car, our brave faces collapsed, and we hugged and wept again. A car drove past slowly. It was our pursuer from the first night. But at least he had the good grace not to stop and ask us how we felt.

We drove on and on, round and round the New Forest. Mike usually enjoys driving – and on this day it became therapeutic for us both. Several times we stopped for an hour or more, and talked. It was dusk when we found ourselves outside the vicarage. We both knew we would have to address the business of a funeral – and we had simultaneously thought of Louise's vicar, Fred. We were both worried that we might be turned away, since we were neither locals, nor churchgoers.

'Well, let's try him, and see what he says,' said Mike. And we rang the doorbell.

It seemed like ages before we heard the tread of his feet, and then the sound of the doorcatch being fumbled. Fred stood in the doorway, his kindly face bathed in warm light. I saw immediately that he had a hole in the toe of his socks.

'Yes?' he said. But we didn't have to say anything. He knew us. His face fell sad and he held out his arms wide. It was as though someone had sent us.

'Come in,' he welcomed. 'Excuse my socks, won't you?'

To us, Fred was an extremely practical man. He was compassionate, sympathetic and warm. But he did not offer us any reason for Supi's death – and we did not ask him why his God had done it. Instead, he gave us vital advice on what to do next, how to arrange a cremation (I couldn't bear the thought of Supi being buried), and he agreed to do the funeral. He sent us away with a list of things to do – from arranging transport to choosing hymns.

Chapter 11

Jon Roseman was on the phone as soon as we were back in our London home. 'The papers have all been on to me,' he said. 'They all want to know where and when the funeral is going to be. What do we tell them?'

'We tell them it's private,' said Mike, firmly.

But that didn't satisfy them. Later Jon returned, this time in some distress...

'They say if you don't tell them where the funeral is, they will make it their business to find out. And it sounded more like a threat than a promise.'

'Who is doing the threatening?'

'The *Sun*,' said Jon. 'And I think they mean it.'

We remembered that the media had almost ruined the funeral of Eric Clapton's little boy. In their frenzy to get a close-up picture, they had pushed and jostled the mourners, and trampled on other graves. We dreaded that. Mike consulted a friend who had once been a Fleet Street editor. He advised us to write personally to every editor, and plead with them to stay away, stressing that we wanted privacy. He said they would be bound to comply in the present climate. They were worried about the increasing likelihood of the government passing a privacy law.

So we wrote to every editor – and it's fair to say that every editor duly concurred. Except that, at the *Sun*, our plea was like a red rag to a raging bull. They weren't going to let that stop them. They would find a way to get what they wanted.

Mike was on the phone to the coroner's office, asking them what was going on. We were shocked to find that, though they had taken Supi's body away at the end of Friday morning, they had not performed the autopsy until Monday. I had thought they had rushed his body away, so that they could immediately perform a post-mortem and find out what had killed him. But they had left him on a cold slab all through the weekend. Surely some vital evidence of disease or illness might have disappeared by then?

This was just the start of my anger, an anger which was to stay with me through the busy months ahead. Why had no-one come to inspect his bedding, his cot, his bedroom? Why hadn't we been asked detailed questions about his health, and his demeanour? Or the health of the rest of us? Why hadn't someone come to take temperature readings? I hadn't even been asked whether he was breast- or bottle-fed. Was no-one interested in why he died?

'We should hear from the pathologist later today,' said Mike.

By early afternoon, the pathologist rang again to confirm that it was Sudden Infant Death Syndrome – that is, that the child has died suddenly and unexpectedly of no known cause. It is a diagnosis of exclusion. It tells you what they know he didn't die from. It rules out murder, and obvious illness or disease. My old friend, Dave Edwards, the paediatrician who had helped us with Jamie, came over to our house – and told us everything he knew about cot death. 'Which is very little,' he admitted. His work was mainly with premature babies – his particular expertise did not stretch to the fortunes of the baby once it had been home for four months.

'Very little is known about cot death at all,' he said. 'There is a fair bit of research going on, but it's making slow progress. We do know that overheating may have something to do with it. And God knows whether there's anything in this theory about cot mattresses.'

I made a mental check on those points. Yes, it had been a hot night, but Supi had been wearing only a T-shirt and a nappy – and his bedroom window was open. It was hardly what you'd call too hot. And yes, I'd bought a brand new mattress. So what could have caused Supi to die? What about this theory that babies simply forget to breathe?

'I don't think it's that simplistic,' said Dave. 'But I'm sorry. I feel useless to you. I don't know why he died. I just don't know.'

Friends came to visit. Neighbours brought notes and posies of flowers. My sister Louise came over from France. At one point, we had so many people – all good friends – in the house, that several of the men got together and went out to buy a Chinese take-away meal. We sat in a group in the playroom, eating with chopsticks from the foil cartons. Before long, someone said something funny and we all laughed. Then, a string of jokes, some of them quite grim. The doorbell rang. Tony, the PR adviser, and Jason – whom I'd worked with at TV-am – came in. I remember the look of shock on their faces. They had come to pay their deepest respects to a family who had just lost their son. And they were greeted with hoots of laughter and the clattering of chopsticks. I felt instantly ashamed – and then realized that we were all too tired, too exhausted, too cried-out to care. And that in the midst of grief, there truly is plenty of laughter, albeit slightly hysterical.

On Day Four, something happened which was to trigger my impatience with the medical world, and its apparent conspiracy of complacency. It was the day when I thought we were all going to die. Mike's parents had come over, and we were playing with the children in the garden. Mike had started to build a fence at one end of the lawn. It was a job he'd been meaning to do for years. I sat in the shade.

Jamie trotted over to me, his face pale.

'Mummy, I feel sick.'

I sat him on my knee and felt his forehead. He was very hot. Suddenly, he vomited all over the grass. He fell back into my arms, and went limp.

'Mike!' I screamed. 'There's something wrong with Jamie!'

We were tending to Jamie when Oliver, in a ghastly copy of his brother, did the same thing – vomited, and almost fainted in a heap on the lawn.

I could feel my heart thumping with panic. 'Oh, my God. We've all got some terrible disease. Whatever killed Supi is going to kill them, too. We're all going to die...'

I raced for the phone, and called Dave Edwards (our paediatrician friend). Luckily his hospital was near – and he was with us quickly. I was still shaking with fear when he summed up.

'Look, I've given them both a thorough examination,' he said, slowly and firmly. He knew now that he was dealing with two very frightened people. 'They are not going to die, all right?' he paused, and clearly saw in our faces the need to say it again. 'They are not going to die. What they've got is ordinary, plain, straight-forward chicken-pox. A bit of Calpol to keep their temperatures down, and they'll be as right as rain in a few days – and then you'll just have the spots to contend with...'

By now, that was not enough for me. I wanted to know more. What exactly was chicken-pox? How did it spread? What did it do to you? And what could it do to a tiny baby, if a tiny baby caught it?

'Now, don't go getting the idea that chicken-pox is the cause of cot death,' said Dave, almost laughingly. 'It is not. Chicken-pox is a virus – and cot death isn't.'

But could a virus play a part in cot death? Already the germ of impatience was beginning to grow inside me. Why did everything the doctors say beg another question – which they were almost reluctant to answer or investigate?

If he'd wanted to get away quickly, I'm afraid Dave didn't that afternoon. He stayed several hours, and ended up on the floor, drawing on scraps of paper diagrams of viruses, hearts, lungs and blood circulatory systems.

When he'd gone, I turned to Mike. 'Shall we ring up the pathologist tomorrow, first thing?'

Mike nodded. 'And ask if there was any trace of chicken-pox in Supi's body? Absolutely!'

While our old friend and GP, Peter Wheeler, had found it hard to cope with the tragedy, our NHS doctor came around several times, to check up on us. This time, she came to see how the boys were progressing with the chicken-pox. Sure enough, the spots were now coming through in an unsightly and very sore rash. I told her that we'd been speaking to the pathologist, and asked him to look for evidence of chicken-pox in the baby.

I had expected her to be supportive. Instead she seemed angry with me. 'What are you doing talking to the pathologist direct?' she railed. 'You'll just upset yourself. You really mustn't do that. It's not good for either of you to go probing about in such matters. You're just torturing yourselves.'

I couldn't believe my ears. It was our child who had died. And I wanted to find out why. In my business, journalism, there was only one way to find the truth quickly – and that was to speak directly to the people concerned. Why shouldn't we speak to the pathologist?

'Don't you think it might be important?' I asked her.

'Chicken-pox has got nothing to do with cot death,' she said. 'And, anyway, all traces of virus will have disappeared by now. That will have gone some six or seven hours after death.'

I was stunned. How could a medical mind be so closed? And why had they left Supi's autopsy until three days after his death, and until vital evidence, like viruses, were untraceable?

Mike rang the pathologist again. He was told that our NHS doctor had been in touch, and they now thought it unwise to speak directly to us. We didn't persist. What was the point? They had ruled out infanticide, obvious disease or illness. That was their job done. There was no 'protocol' for them to search any further. Verdict – Sudden Infant Death Syndrome. In other words, we don't know what killed your baby. As long as we know it wasn't murder or negligence, that's all right by us. SIDS effectively stands for Hard Luck This Time. Cheer Up And Have Another One. It is, quite literally, an excuse for a verdict.

Nowhere, it seemed to us, was there a doctor who was in the least bit curious, let alone caring about what had happened to our baby. And there was another thing: it had said in one of the newspaper reports about us that four or five babies died from SIDS every day. Did that really mean that, on the morning our world turned upside down, the same mind-numbing tragedy had hit the hearts of four or five other families?

It was barely believable. Because that meant over twenty a week. Over 2,000 a year. Healthy, bonny babies. (Because by the very definition of cot death, it happens to lively, healthy babies.)

Two thousand? How come we had never heard about it? How come there wasn't an enormous government inquiry? How come there weren't questions asked in the House? How come it wasn't a national scandal?

How could we simply accept it? What was wrong with us all? How come so many people had patted us on the back and told us to go away and have another one? Is it because he was a baby?

If, every year in this country, 2,000 young adults were found mysteriously dead in their beds from something called Sudden Adult Death Syndrome, wouldn't there be a national emergency declared? What the hell was going on in this civilized country of ours?

With Shirley, I went down to the headquarters of the Foundation for the Study of Infant Deaths, to thank them for the wonder of their leaflet, which had been so helpful. And to ask them what had killed my baby. We met Joyce Epstein, the director, who had been in her job only about six months. With her was Dr Shireen Chantler, a scientist and secretary of the Foundation's scientific advisory committee.

They were kind and sympathetic, and offered coffee. They told me how the Foundation had been set up, after a cot death twenty-one years before. The child's mother had found that nothing was being done to investigate the cause of SIDS, and vowed to do something about it. As I sat in their lofty office, drinking their tea, it seemed to me, perhaps unfairly, that very little progress had been made in the last twenty-one years.

'The government does next to nothing about cot death,' said Joyce in her clipped Canadian accent. 'The Foundation raises millions of pounds, and funds masses of scientific projects. Progress is being made – but we're still a long way off finding the cause.'

For the first time, I was talking to someone who knew about cot death. And yet it kept nagging me how little was known. They told me that they were worried about the future. Fundraising was becoming more and more difficult. And if the Foundation ran out of money, the research projects would have to stop.

'I hope you don't mind my saying,' said Dr Chantler. 'But you're the best thing that's ever happened to cot death.'

Joyce Epstein shot her an angry look. But it was all right. I understood what she meant. She was, after all, a research doctor and not a bereaved mother.

'Tell me,' she asked quietly, as I was preparing to leave. 'Was your baby sleeping on his stomach?'

I responded immediately – lest there be any doubt he was in the safest position of all. 'Yes, all my babies have slept on their tummy,' I said. 'Why?'

'Well,' said Dr Chantler, looking concerned. 'There has been some research into sleeping position – but we don't know very much about it yet...'

We left, armed with a couple of videos and a handful of books.

'It's good to talk to someone who understands,' Shirley said.

'Yes, but they can't bring Supi back, can they?' I replied. In truth, I had found the pair of them a bit creepy. And, somehow, it had annoyed me that they were running an organization about cot death when neither of them had any personal experience of it. Their professional calm had irritated me. This was not a calm situation – it was raw, stinging torture – and I needed the solace of other mums who really did know how it felt.

Mercifully, they were already putting pen to paper.

Chapter 12

Every morning, from Day One, letters came tumbling through our letterbox. I don't know how I would have got through the day without them. We heard from friends we had almost forgotten, old colleagues in TV and radio stations all around the world, and celebrity names who offered their status to help raise funds for cot death research. But in an even greater number came the long letters from total strangers. Yet now we had more in common with them than the others, because, they, too, had lost a child to cot death. They were the people who could say 'I know how you feel' and really mean it. In their hundreds, they wrote to 'Anne Diamond, LONDON,' to tell us both that they understood the agony we were enduring, the sense of hopelessness, of betrayal, the feeling that life was no longer worth living.

But there was one particular letter I was waiting for. I almost sat by the front door willing it to come. It didn't materialize on the first day after Supi's death, nor the second, nor the third. But it came on the fourth – and I drank in its every word, trembling as I read it.

It was the letter from Clare Richards. I just knew she would write. Clare had been a producer at TV-am when I was working on *Good Morning Britain*. She was a highly intelligent, bright bubbly girl, full of drive and enthusiasm for her job. I didn't know her particularly well, but I remember the office buzz when she started to bulge, and then announced to everyone that she was pregnant. Everyone was delighted for her and her husband, Hugh.

Clare left work to have her baby, and expected to take her

full six months' maternity leave before coming back. So it was a shock to find her back at work just a couple of months later. Her beautiful, and totally healthy baby, Harriet, had died of cot death.

Clare had taken the baby to see her mum. She had laid Harriet down on her mother's bed, and the two women had left the baby sleeping peacefully while they made lunch downstairs. Twenty minutes later, when Clare went to check, she found Harriet dead. They tried everything – shaking her, mouth to mouth resuscitation, all to no avail.

The whole office was talking about it, in hushed tones. I don't think I had the courage even to go up to Clare and offer my sympathy. At that time, I didn't understand babies, let alone the agony of losing one. But when Clare later asked me to support a fund-raising event for cot death research at her home town, I gladly agreed.

Now, I knew I needed Clare's advice. And she wrote a long letter. Later I visited Clare at her home. It was good to see her again, though desperately sad. Where we had hardly known each other as colleagues, we were now united in our separate experience of grief.

Harriet had been just one month old – and a girl. Fairly unusual for cot death, Clare explained. The 'classic' cases of cot death tended to be boys, often with a history of prematurity, and the most common age was four and a half months. So Supi was a 'classic'.

Clare had only two pictures of Harriet – and they were quite distant shots of her, taken by a neighbour. Everything they had belonging to her, including their own personal pictures of her, had been burned in an accidental fire at their house.

'But that's all right, I have my memories,' said Clare. She said that she, too, had wanted to know more about cot death, to ask why Harriet had died. 'But,' she warned me, 'be careful not to become obsessed with his death. I was advised from the beginning not to make Harriet's death bigger than her life. And it's her life I now remember.'

Clare had gone on to have another child, a boy. 'I look upon him as my gift from Harriet,' she said. 'Because, if she had lived, I'm sure we would never have gone on to have him.' She now has two gifts from Harriet.

Many, many letters came from Ireland. And Mass cards. It seemed that on the Sundays immediately following Supi's death, hundreds of masses were said for him, especially throughout Ireland.

One letter was from a couple who had lost their baby daughter, Sorcha, on exactly the same day one year before. They had been suffering their own private agony, marking the first anniversary of her death, when they heard on the news that Anne Diamond, the British TV star, had lost her baby son to cot death.

And this one, from my old TV-am mate and footballing star, Jimmy Greaves, gave us quite a shock:

Dear Anne and Mike,

Our deepest sympathy to you both for what has happened.

Irene and I suffered the same fate in 1958. I can only say time heals but in the meantime our thoughts are with you,

Yours very sincerely,

Jim and Irene Greaves.

It was a fact about Jimmy Greaves that even his greatest football fans hadn't known. Their first son, little Jimmy, had died of cot death. He, too, had been a 'classic' case – a four-month-old boy.

Just a few weeks before Supi died, we had taken all three of our children to a favourite annual bash – Esther Rantzen's birthday party. Esther often held a large gathering in the rambling grounds of her country home in Hampshire. Most of the BBC and half of ITV would be there – famous faces and infamous names, together with some of the most influential producers, directors and controllers. It was always a good afternoon. So, even with a small baby and all his paraphernalia in tow, we joined in the fun. Now we received letters from many people who had been there, and who had met him:

Dear Anne,

I am Esther's cousin. And I had the pleasure of
meeting you and your sons at her birthday party last
month. My daughters were in the swimming pool with
your boys.
I was very sorry indeed to hear about the death
of your baby. He gave me a lovely smile that
afternoon and even made me feel broody. No doubt he
gave a lot of pleasure to many people in his short life.

It was a lovely letter to receive – because it spoke of Supi's life, not just of his death. Months later, when Mike and I were at a party given by Jeffrey Archer, the millionaire novelist, I remembered a conversation I had with a prominent politician's wife. 'I was so sorry about your baby,' she said to me. 'He looked absolutely beautiful.' It mattered so much to me that she had added that last comment. I knew he was gorgeous – but now I needed to hear it from others, too.

We even got a letter from the people who used to live in our house:

Dear Anne,

As a mother of two baby boys myself, I cannot
imagine how you must feel – but I feel even more
appalled that such a wonderfully happy house could
allow this to happen, because I lived there with my

114

family for sixteen wonderful years, and am deeply
shocked.

With very best wishes,

Vicky Isow

Claire Rayner sent a lovely letter, and offered her unique
help, should we want to talk. Jilly Cooper immediately sent us
a letter of sympathy, entreating us to eat properly and take lots
of Vitamin C – 'it sounds banal, but it does help because the
flip side of a shock like this is utter, numbing exhaustion.'
A short note came from the Wirral. It said:

Just to say we're all thinking of you up here. Love,
Mike McCartney and family.

I had met Paul's brother a few years before, and all we'd
talked about then was kids.
From Cyprus, a fax from John and Roswitha at the Bunch
of Grapes:

Words are nothing. They cannot express our feelings.
Please understand that. We don't want to elaborate
in words. But we all want to tell you 'God bless you
all' and give you the strength to accept his will.

'My heart aches for you,' wrote Gay, who had been my wonderful and faithful secretary during my years at TV-am:

Only parents could begin to know the despair and
sorrow you feel. Poor loveable little Supi – and
poor Ollie and Jamie. How they will miss him and not
understand and ask painful, heartbreaking questions.
I wish so much that I could comfort you. What a

115

terrible sadness for everyone.

But I know that you are both strong and devoted loving parents and you will find some way to carry on in spite of the terrible ache you feel inside.

I'm thinking about you all the time and hoping and praying that you may find a way to lessen your pain.

Many of our friends had learned the news from reporters, who'd phoned them to ask for their reaction. My old sofa-mate, presenter Mike Morris, wrote:

Sometimes words fail even a so-called communicator. I first heard about your tragedy when a man I'd never heard of phoned me at home. 'Who do you work for?' I asked. 'The *Sun*,' he said.

T'was ever thus. I gulped and said : 'Hold on a moment... I can't gather my thoughts.' For some reason one phrase crossed my brain: 'She's a fighter.' I knew the phrase was right but in my tiredness (you know all about that!) I was terrified that it was inappropriate. I still don't know the answer. I know that you're brave and I hope to God that helps.

No honeyed words of assurance will fill the vacuum or erase the vision you must have suffered. Even the comforting arm around the shoulder will make you temporarily weaker. Even time itself will not heal. It will, however, make the scar less vivid.

All I can say is that if you ever want a temporary haven or a quiet afternoon or even complete silence, please regard my home as a possibility. When you have lived through madness sometimes only a fellow madman can begin to comprehend. Please give my regards to Mike as the two of you search for strength over the next few months.

Yours, with love and admiration,

Mike Morris

I had always known he had a heart of gold, but I had never thought him quite so eloquent. I read his letter and cried. It just proved to me how close a team we all had been at the breakfast station, particularly the original few who had kept the station going in its first few turbulent months. Many of them sent wonderful letters, including Greg Dyke – the man they called the station's saviour. And delivered to our door by special messenger came a heartfelt note from Bruce Gyngell. I knew he would be hurting badly for us.

So many people sent poems, I could have compiled an anthology. Many were overtly religious – or offered philosophical explanations I was not ready for.

Anne Robbins, a TV-am viewer from Yorkshire, must have started composing as soon as she heard the news:

> The crib that held your little one
> Is empty now – your child has gone
> And yet he's but a breath away
> His love's around you every day.
>
> He chose to spend his life with you
> He knew that time was precious too.
> He gave to you a lifetime's love,
> Now he lives with God above.
>
> Just be thankful for all the joy
> Brought to you from this little boy.
> Some never know a baby's smile
> You were blest for a little while.

So dry your eyes and weep no more
Love the ones that were born before
You and the babe will never part
He lives forever in your heart.

Ed and Amanda Watkins wrote from their home in Belper in Derbyshire:

Words cannot express the feelings that we share with you. I have heard that so many times, and by now, so must you have done.

We lost our daughter, Stephanie, in May this year, although still very recent and at times, painful, we have found that we can carry on. Given time, I promise you both you will smile again, you will laugh, and you will not feel guilty. If you want to speak to somebody who is not famous, not an expert, but who is going 'through it', don't hesitate to ring or write or just turn up. Others have helped us so perhaps we can help you, just a little.

Take care and love each other.

So many people seemed to be frightened that the intensity of our grief might drive Mike and me apart. It happened to one woman, who wrote an anguished letter:

Dear Anne and Mike,

I feel compelled to write to you, firstly to say how sad and helpless I feel for you both and secondly to tell you of my experience in the hope that perhaps if you read this letter you may not suffer as much as I have.

My first child, a daughter called Amy, was born on 17 October 1980. I was twenty-seven years old, I was married to my second husband and everything seemed rosy.

We had three months with my darling Amy. Then it happened. 14 January 1981. That date will be engraved on my memory for as long as I live. Amy was fine that morning but by 4pm she was dead. I had been out in the car with her, and then I carried her carrycot indoors. Amy was sleeping peacefully and I put her into the bedroom while I wrote a letter. By about 4pm I thought I'd wake Amy for a feed. I picked her up (mumbling something about her being a little lazy-bones, as you do!) and I knew instantly. The look on her face will be with me forever. I had lost my Amy and there was nothing I could do about it.

I know you will feel grief, pain, guilt, frustration, hate and all the other negative emotions. In some ways I think the fact that Amy was our first child may have been a blessing. I was completely incapable of giving love to anyone, and my husband suffered dreadfully.

He tried to comfort me through those awful first weeks, but I felt so bad I didn't want comfort. I did not want to feel better, so I shunned his attention. I refused to let him help me.

We contemplated suicide, things got so bad. I can remember one evening, I'd been crying all day. We were just about to go to bed and I told my husband I could not face another day. I didn't want to wake up in the morning. We actually discussed ways we could do it.

I spent my days swallowed up in grief. I wouldn't speak to anyone. My friends would phone but I wouldn't answer the phone and my husband had to cope with all of that.

Thinking about it now I suppose I was pretty selfish. My husband was suffering, too, and I was probably making things worse. I shut myself away with memories of Amy and there I stayed.

Thankfully I became pregnant the next month and that pregnancy was what kept me going. I still felt the same but I had to keep going for the new baby. I desperately wanted another girl.

My relationship with my husband had deteriorated, I continued to go it alone. Of course, I never realized what I was doing at the time.

Lindsay was born in November 1981. Although at the time we were overjoyed, her birth brought new problems and pressures. As you can imagine, we watched her like a hawk. Took it in turns to watch her twenty-four hours a day.

After the three months hurdle had passed, things got a little easier, although I became pregnant again – so physically I was shattered and probably mentally, too, as I still hadn't come to terms with Amy's death.

Ten years on, I have two beautiful healthy children who are very special to me. Sadly I am divorced from my husband because the gap between us could not be overcome.

This morning, the children have gone on holiday with their father and I am very tearful.

I've made so many mistakes. Things could have been so different. I hope you will share each other's grief. Give each other the comfort you so badly need and accept it gladly. Most important of all, don't bottle anything up inside. Tell each other every thought and feeling, however bad. Cry and grieve, talk about Sebastian but don't forget your love for each other and your children. You might think it couldn't happen to you, but take it from someone who let it happen to her.

Time is the greatest healer. I remember someone saying that to me, and thinking they don't know what they're talking about. I'll never get over Amy. Never feel better. But it is true I'll never forget Amy. I love her dearly and always will. I still weep for her especially on her birthday. I fill the house with flowers and find it hard to cope that day.

Her pictures are around the house and I can now look at them and smile – something I thought I'd never be able to do.

I hope very much that this letter will bring you some kind of comfort. It will be a long, long road back to any kind of normality, but you will get there eventually – and together, I hope.

Yours sincerely,

Helen Hill

PS. Life is eternal and love is immortal
and death is only an horizon,
and an horizon is nothing
save the limit of our sight.

'Dear Anne and Mike' [wrote Vivienne Richardson from Northern Ireland]:

My heart goes out to you. I know exactly how you are feeling. David and myself have lost four children – all boys. Three just after birth, and one miscarriage at twelve weeks. Please don't forget about your other sons, they need you also – don't be afraid to cry with them. Mike will feel a bit left out because people always ask how mum is – forgetting that dad had any part at all.

I believe my sons were taken for a reason only God knows. I know we will meet them again some day –

even though I would rather have them here now. We have a six-year-old daughter, Victoria, whom we treasure. We can't have any more because my womb burst, lung collapsed and I had a clot on my heart. I ended up with my womb being removed.

I know you'll never get over this but the pain gets easier, and as someone said to me – Heaven would be a very lonely place without children!

He is being well looked after and we will meet our sons again.

I am not a Bible thumper but I do believe in God and in Heaven. I do hope your family will find peace soon, Love and God Bless...

After my abortive conversation with the voice on the phone at the local Catholic church, I was surprised but very comforted to receive a note from the priest who had been out on the morning of Supi's death:

Dear Mr and Mrs Hollingsworth,

May I just give first and foremost my deepest condolences on your tragic loss, and assure you of my prayers.

I am very sorry that neither Father Tom nor myself were here when you called. I returned only this afternoon (I am a school chaplain) and I came round and discovered a considerable number of press people camped near your door. Rather than publicly intrude on private grief, I felt that it would be better to write than to in any way add to the pain.

Please find small comfort in faith, and believe that God does not create to destroy. Your child, though taken from you, is alive and well and with Him, in whom all hope and faith is founded...

I was pleased that he'd written. And glad that he had put two and two together (because, I realized, I'd never told the voice who we were or where) and come around. Of course, by then, James had reached us. But I was sad, too, that he hadn't knocked on our door. Because we might still have needed him. Maybe even priests, as well as doctors, policemen and other officials, need more instruction on bereavement care.

One letter was a small parcel. It contained a book called *Coping with Cot Death* (Sheldon Press). In it there was a short letter from the author, Sarah Murphy:

Dear Anne and Mike,

I have hesitated about sending you a copy of my book for fear of intruding. But remembering how isolated we felt following the cot death of our three-month-old daughter Elizabeth, even though we were surrounded by friends, I've decided to risk sending it and hope that you won't feel offended.

I was so very sorry to hear about Sebastian's sudden death. I help to run our local support group in Brighton and Hove and I remember you coming to the James Bond première, Anne, to help raise funds for research into cot death.

Having tried actively to prevent such deaths, the irony of what has just happened to you is not lost upon me.

Please accept my very best wishes to you all, and I hope that my book may be of some help to you.

It was. I took the book back to bed with me that morning, and read it from cover to cover within two hours. It is the best, and most constructive, book I have ever read on the subject of cot death and bereavement. I immediately felt some small sense of recovery. As though, one day, there might be light at the end of this painfully dark tunnel. And I also felt some strange kinship with this extraordinary woman who had been through what I was going through.

Several months later I was opening a dolls' house fair in Brighton, to raise funds for research. On my way out of the hall, a slim woman came up to me in the crowd. 'I'm Sarah Murphy,' she said. I wanted to fling my arms around her. At her side was her daughter Mary, almost a teenager – the twin sister of the baby who had died. The emotion of meeting her was almost too much to bear, in front of such a crowd and with my best 'personal appearance' suit on.

Sarah's book is a must for anyone who has lost a child. I regularly lend my copy to people who are bereaved, and not just by cot death. She, too, wrote a poem shortly after Elizabeth's death:

Elizabeth

I thought I could swim but I find I can barely tread water.
I relive that morning – no warning, so well and so real:
I bathed you and dressed you and fed you, no danger in
    daytime –
The thought of you gnaws at a rawness that time does not
    heal.

At lunchtime, your pram in the sunshine, the radio talking.
I went out to check you and saw you were sleeping,
    content.
The phone went – a friend: could she visit? I hastily tidied,
She came and we chattered and frittered the half-hour we
    spent.

The binmen came, clattering lids, and I went out to check
    you –
Dead . . . you were dead . . . you were dead, oh dear God,
    you were dead.
How could our cord have been cut with no slice of the
    knifeblade?

124

Me seven months pregnant with Supi – and just before the problems of polyhydramnios set in, causing me to go into labour four weeks early.

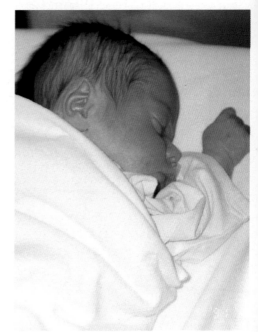

This was the shot we used on the front of Supi's birth announcement. Ironically, he is of course, happily asleep on his tummy.

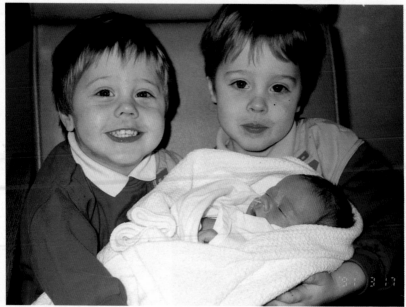

Oliver and Jamie were thrilled to hold their younger brother for the very first time, as soon as he was allowed out of special care.

Some people think that cot death babies are weak little things. This picture of Supi with Oliver proves that he was a loving, living member of the family and full of character.

Mum and Sebastian at the Bunch of Grapes in Cyprus. He was beginning to get a bit tetchy, so we set off home.

Just as we were leaving the Bunch of Grapes, Alex stopped us and took this photo. It's the only shot I have of the five of us together as a family. I will always be grateful she took it, even though I didn't think to turn Sebastian round, so we could see his face.

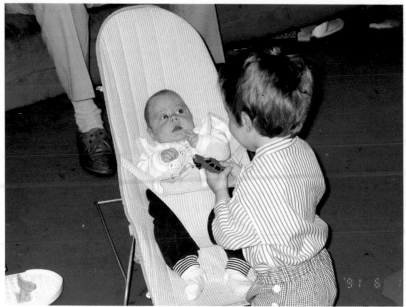

Jamie with Supi. Supi was usually the centre of attention, 'chairing' events from his bouncy chair in the middle of the room.

Supi and Mike had a special relationship.

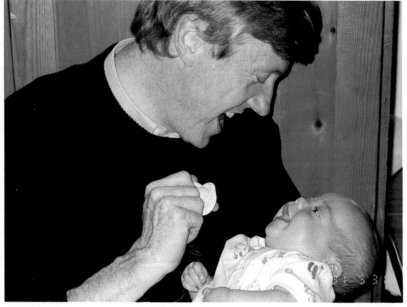

The *Sun's* front page on the morning after the funeral. Contrary to some reports, we had asked every newspaper to stay away – with no exceptions. But the *Sun* still managed to get this shot.

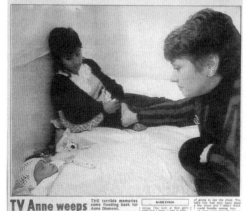

The morning I met another cot death mother – a 16-year-old Maori girl and her tiny dead son. This picture came from the documentary and was released to the press.

The New Zealand expedition team – Alex, Shirley, me, Oliver, Mike and Jamie. The boys felt they were part of the mission to find out what had killed their baby brother.

Mrs Virginia Bottomley, then Health Minister, and me on the day the Back to Sleep campaign was launched – 'the most successful health campaign ever'. (© *Express Newspapers*)

The 'Back to Sleep' poster. A great slogan, but the artwork was rather confusing and some people read it as 'ack to Sleep' and wondered what it meant!

The launch of the Health Education Authority campaign highlighting the dangers of smoking to babies (© *Peter Trievnor/Times Newspapers Limited*)

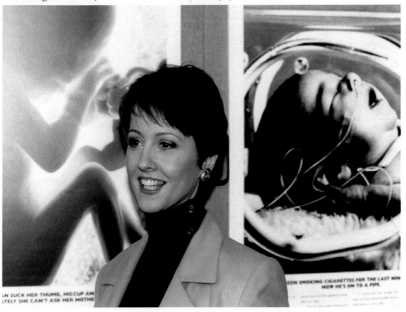

At every month of Jake's life we felt another milestone had been passed – so we celebrated each month with a birthday cake. This was his sixth!

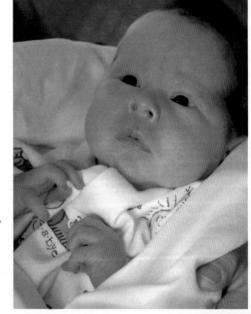

And finally, the fifth son, Conor Joe, who was born four years after Supi, almost to the day. Now, as everyone joked on the congratulations cards, we have our five-a-side football team – though one member will always be missing.

Life doesn't end at three months when your whole life's
  ahead.

You died so alone yet so near and it buffets like breakers.
I should have been with you, it drags at me, tugging me
  down.
I'm only afloat with the rafters of friends and my family –
It's hard to stay surfaced when part of you's wanting to
  drown.

The binmen are clattering lids and the radio's talking.
Thursday, the day that you died, and a year has gone by.
Groundless, I'm floundering, wounded yet walking – in
  water
That thwarts with the not-knowing-how and the not-
  knowing-why.

Acceptance will come, there's so much that we can't
  understand.
In the grief of this world what's the measure of one baby
  daughter?
I still have belief, the sea's calmer; I know I'll reach land.
But I thought I could swim and I find I can barely tread
  water.

As Sarah's letter had made a dramatic impact upon me, so
Mike was deeply moved by a letter he received from another
bereaved father. He was called Anton Simon – and he told
Mike how he and his wife, Tess, had lost their baby son, Harry,
only a couple of months before. He described how every sub-
sequent action, every mouthful of food, every trivial chore of
everyday life now felt like a betrayal of Harry. Like us, they
couldn't conceive of how life could possibly go on.

His words struck such a chord with Mike that he wrote
back, and within days, Tess and Anton phoned us. We all

talked on the telephone for what must have been hours, crying, comparing anxieties, worries, feelings of guilt. They sent us an extract from Charles Dickens's *The Old Curiosity Shop*. I keep it in my purse – so that it is always handy. Because if anyone understood children, and fought to turn our society into one which cared more for little ones, then it was Dickens. As a loving father, he, too, knew the pain of losing a child. He wrote this after describing the death of little Nell:

> Oh! it is hard to take to heart the lesson that such deaths will teach, but let no man reject it, for it is one that all must learn, and is a mighty, universal Truth. When Death strikes down the innocent and young, for every fragile form from which he lets the panting spirit free, a hundred virtues rise, in shapes of mercy, charity, and love, to walk the world, and bless it. Of every tear that sorrowing mortals shed on such green graves, some good is born, some gentler nature comes. In the Destroyer's steps there spring up bright creations that defy his power, and his dark path becomes a way of light to Heaven.

Tess and Anton, although we have never met them, stay close in our hearts. We still write occasionally – but they are more often in my thoughts. And Harry's name is one of the many in my heart, whenever I do something in the fight against cot death. Or when I light a candle.

A friend once told me that he didn't know what he felt about religion – but he was sure of one thing: 'If there is a Heaven – then to a child it must be some sort of giant Disneyland. And if that is so, then Sebastian is already on the rides!' I like that. And there's another thing. If Supi is there, then he is with a lot of little friends.

126

Chapter 13

Supi came home in a little snow-white coffin. Mike carried him upstairs to his own room and laid the casket in the cot. We both wanted him to stay there one more night, before the funeral the next day. But the sight of him, waxen-faced and doll-like, dressed in his summery Cyprus outfit, lying on his fleecy sheepskin, in a white coffin, in a white cot, served to underline the illogicality of his death. That he should be lying dead among so much softness, comfort, baby-whiteness, seemed an affront to nature.

Alex asked if she could see him. I took her into his room and lifted the top off his coffin.

'He doesn't really look like Supi,' she said quietly. And she was right. He didn't. Although the funeral parlour had been very sensitive with the make-up, his face was quite the wrong colour. And to try and hide the purple lips, they had lightly dabbed him with orangey lipstick. In a way, it helped. It emphasized to me that our child, our delightful little gurgling baby son, was not there. This was simply his body – and we had to 'do right by him'. But his spirit was no longer there.

My eyes always looked up to the sash window whenever I thought of where he had gone. Do spirits soar, as I had been taught in my Catholic teachings? Had he flown into the warm, summer night? Or had his energy been absorbed into the very fabric of the walls around us?

'A coffin in a cot,' I said to Alex, shaking my head. 'I hope you never see such a sight again.'

I did not lift him out. I was too frightened of discovering on his body, on his head, the marks of the pathologist's knife.

Besides, I had held him so long on the morning of his death, I didn't think I could again bear the unnatural feeling of a cold baby. I wanted to remember him warm with life.

We had resolved not to tell the children any more than the very simple explanation that Supi had 'gone to Heaven'. We sensed that, at just four and two years old, they would accept that for the present. We wanted them to come to the funeral service – so we had to explain the casket, which we said was a box of messages and flowers which we were sending to Supi in Heaven. We were careful not to let slip any remark that might betray the truth that Supi's body was in there. I thought that the truth would be too awful for them to comprehend, especially since we were opting for a cremation afterwards.

Planning a funeral service certainly helps concentrate the mind. It's undoubtedly a ritual designed to get you through those first few awful days when you are beyond comfort – and have not yet achieved acceptance. Should we have music? Both Mike and I wanted simplicity, and something childlike. So we chose 'The Lord's My Shepherd' and 'Jesus, Good Above All Other', a hymn I had loved since primary school.

Should we have a choir? Again, I wanted things kept simple – so my first reaction was no. But one of Mike's favourite pieces of music was the 'Nunc Dimittis' by Geoffrey Burgon which was sung at the end of the TV series, *Tinker, Tailor, Soldier, Spy*. We wondered if we should have the record played in the church. But Shirley, herself a former singer with a great many influential musical friends, thought she could do better...

'Please, *please* let me try and find a choirboy!'

I laughed. *Yes, you do laugh even though you're planning the funeral of your own son.* 'You'll never find one who can sing that. It's a pretty obscure piece of music. And it's got all sorts of difficult orchestral bits in it, too...'

'Just give me a chance,' insisted Shirley, and she hit the phones. Several hours later, she came to find us, looking very pleased with herself. 'You'll never guess who lives in Bournemouth,' she started.

We looked puzzled.

'Only the runner-up to Choirboy of the Year!' she smiled. 'I've spoken to his dad, who will accompany him, and they do know Mike's favourite 'Nunc Dimittis'. What's more, they want to know if you'd like a trumpeter, because they know one who can do it...'

Mike and I sat down at the dining-room table, and together composed a letter to Supi. We cried, and hugged, and made endless cups of tea – none of which we drank – and we worked into the small hours. This was the letter which we then placed with him:

Dearest Supi,

Today is the day of your funeral and we would like to stand up in church and say how proud we are of you. Neither of us believe we will be able to say anything out loud – so we are writing it down in order that you may at least understand how we feel.

We have to say something. Once we could have expected to sing at your birthday, to applaud at the Nativity Play, to read you bedtime stories, to help and advise, cajole and encourage ...

I thought I would be able to write it all down here, but I can't. It is still too painful to read right through. Maybe it should remain totally private, between Supi and us.

Oliver and Jamie scrawled a note and a picture for him and Alex, too, gave him a special message with a tiny, dried rosebud, tied with a blue ribbon.

So many people said to us afterwards: 'I don't know how you did it. I wouldn't have been able to cope' but Mike and I knew that we *had* to cope. To collapse in shock, as the papers had described me doing, or to lock yourself away in grief, would have been to abandon our parental duty. Now, as much as our duty to nurture our living, healthy children, we felt a responsibility to our little dead son. He badly needed us to help him leave this world with dignity and a vital expression of love.

We also knew, as Fred the vicar had told us, that we would have to live with this day for the rest of our lives. And we should do whatever we felt was needed, so that we could look back upon this day with affection and the knowledge that we did right. So we invited our close family, and friends who had known Supi. Gay, my former secretary, came – and so did Nanny Anne Robinson, who had helped care for him in the first few weeks of his life, my colleague and great friend Nick Owen and his wife Jill – and of course, Shirley.

One morning the phone rang – Mike answered it, and then burst into tears. It was Becky, his daughter from his first marriage. He loved her very much, but she had not spoken to him for two years, after a small row, which had exposed the sensitivities of her feelings after her parents' divorce. She had, therefore, never met Supi. But she had read in the newspapers of his death – and decided to ring her dad. She sent the most beautiful posy of flowers – and later wrote her little lost brother a poem. And she and her father became close again.

Everyone gathered at my parents' bungalow before the service – so when we arrived, the assembly was complete. We put Supi in a bedroom – and those who wanted to could see him. I went in with my sisters. We sat silently around him, on the bed, and stared at his little face, his tiny fingers permanently frozen in a delicate clasp. My sister Sue had written a poem. Her hands trembling as she held the card, and her voice quivering, she read it out to him, then gently placed the card at his side.

It was time to go to the church. The police had been warned that we might have some unwelcome visitors from Fleet Street, but when we arrived there was no sign of anyone. We sighed with relief. Our letters to the editors must have worked. Mike carried the coffin in, past the baptismal font, and down the aisle, past our friends and family in the box pews. He laid it at the altar, among the flowers.

A blonde choirboy, aged about twelve, was sitting near by. I shot him a smile, and he smiled back. It must have been a terribly upsetting experience for him, that day. There was also a man I didn't know at all, sitting in the choir stalls. I had a suspicious mind, borne of many years of trying to anticipate Fleet Street tricks...Could he be a reporter?

Mike and I joined Shirley and Oliver in the front box pew. Alex sat with Jamie behind us. Both boys were quiet and controlled – though I think Jamie's calm was helped along by Alex and a nifty supply of Polo mints.

Through breaking voices, Shirley read 'Suffer Little Children To Come Unto Me' and Nick the poem 'Above the Bright Blue Sky' by Albert Midlane:

> There's a Friend for little children
> Above the bright blue sky,
> A Friend who never changes,
> Whose love will never die;
> Our earthly friends may fail us,
> And change with changing years,
> This Friend is always worthy
> Of that dear name he bears.
>
> There's a home for little children
> Above the bright blue sky,
> Where Jesus reigns in glory,
> A home of peace and joy;
> No home on earth is like it,
> Nor can with it compare;
> And everyone is happy,
> Nor could be happier there.

The choirboy stood for the 'Nunc Dimittis' – and his bright treble voice pierced the heady, almost suffocating atmosphere of overpowering sadness. And then the mystery man stood up – and blew his trumpet. Of course! He wasn't a reporter – he was the trumpeter for the 'Nunc Dimittis'! Shirley and I glanced at each other. She had done well. The music was beautiful.

As we left the church, Mike carrying the coffin and me gripping his arm, Fred whispered in our ears: 'I'm sorry – but there does seem to be a photographer outside...'

We were beyond such matters. By now, with our emotions heightened by the readings and the music, we were in another world, unaware that our grim faces were being snapped on a long lens, and that even small details, such as loading the coffin into the car, were being captured on film.

We followed Fred in his car to the crematorium. And there, as soft organ pipes played in the background, the three of us watched his little casket, crowned with our posy of country flowers, descend to the depths.

My sisters say I was white when I returned to my parents' home. We were both drained. 'Our little Supi had a trumpeter,' I repeated again and again, to anyone who'd listen. 'Our little boy had a trumpeter...'

We laid out all his flowers on the lawn. My sister Sue took flowers from each posy and bouquet to make a dried flower basket for us to keep.

'Whose flowers are those?' Mike's mother asked, pointing to one posy.

'They're from Becky,' I said. 'She's back.'

Mike's mother dabbed her eyes. 'That's Supi at work,' she said. 'He's reunited Mike with Becky.' And she glanced at the sofa, where Mike was sitting with Shirley. 'And Supi has brought them back together as well. He's done such a lot of good in his little life.'

Chapter 14

Later that same afternoon, and while we were still wondering how we could live through such pain, Jon Roseman took a phone call. It was from the *Sun*.

'They say they've got a very powerful picture from the funeral and they're going to use it on their front page,' he relayed to us. 'They're asking – will you give them permission to use it?'

Permission? Since when did the *Sun* ever ask for permission to print something about you? Our answer was blunt. 'No,' said Mike. 'We asked everyone to stay away. Tell them no, we most certainly do not give our permission.'

Jon passed the message on – but within half an hour, they had rung him again on his mobile phone. Apologetic at having to discuss the subject at all at such a time, Jon took Mike and me aside again. 'I'm so sorry to have to put you through this,' he said. 'But they insist that I give you the full facts. They say they didn't intrude on your funeral – that they were offered the pictures by a freelance photographer. They say it's a very dramatic and poignant picture of you both carrying the coffin, and they're going to use it to appeal for funds for cot death research. They say they're going to use it anyway – but they would rather do it with your permission.'

Mike snapped. He had been brave and controlled all day. Now his patience was breaking. He turned on Jon and almost shouted: 'They must be bloody worried about being seen to invade our privacy, mustn't they? Yes, I bet they would rather have our permission. That would get them neatly off the hook, wouldn't it? No – they do *not* have our permission. We asked

133

everyone to stay away – and everyone else did. It would be completely wrong for us to sanction them just because they say they're going to do it to raise funds.'

And that's how it was left. We didn't hear from them again. But at least we had been prepared for the shock of seeing the next day's newspaper. Because our picture wasn't just on the front page. It *was* the front page. The headline, in huge type, read: OUR LITTLE LOVE. There were few accompanying words. Simply, and at the very foot of the page, they had printed: 'All donations to the Foundation for the Study of Infant Death, 35 Belgrave Square, London W1.'

It was indeed a very poignant picture. Outrageously intrusive, yes, but undeniably powerful. Together, Mike and I looked at it with mixed feelings. As the people involved, the parents of that child in the little white casket, we were incensed, and tormented, at the invasion of our most private moment. But as television journalists we immediately recognized the impact of a powerful image.

'I'm glad we didn't give them permission, though,' said Mike.

But it wasn't as simple as that. Within twenty-four hours we had become victims of the sniping circulation war within Fleet Street. Again, poor Jon Roseman was fielding calls, this time from an angry *Daily Mirror*, charging us with complicity. They were accusing us of doing a deal with the *Sun*. They assumed we had asked all the other newspapers to stay away, and all the time we had planned to give the *Sun* the exclusive rights to be there at the funeral.

We could barely believe it. We had hardly survived our own child's funeral than we were being accused of something so cheap and tawdry that it threatened to sully his name. We charged Jon with getting back to both newspapers. The *Daily Mirror* were told that they were seriously wrong. The *Sun* were told that they would be quickly and sensationally reported to the Press Commission if they didn't make it clear in the next day's edition that they had acted against our will, and had never received our permission to print. They acquiesced – and made the point clear. In a very small paragraph. At the bottom of a different page.

But, they were right about the impact of that picture. The publicity prompted a flood of calls to the switchboard of the Foundation in London. The Samaritans up and down the country reported that they were deluged with calls from panicking mothers. Bereaved parents were unable to get through to the helplines, which were jammed instead by parents frightened that their babies might suddenly stop breathing.

'We cannot really reassure them,' a spokeswoman told the national newspapers. 'Cot death can strike at any time and cot death babies are healthy right up to their death. There is no known cause for cot death. Parents must trust their instincts and common sense and see a doctor if they are worried. It's a pity it takes a celebrity's baby to die to raise the issue.'

One lady wrote to me when she saw the *Sun*'s front page. It brought home to me how long my grieving might take:

Dear Anne and Mike,

Just a line to say how sorry I was at the tragic death of your little boy. I saw Mike with the little white coffin in the *Sun* paper, and I just burst into tears. It brought back memories of when I carried my little Robert of nine weeks to church to be buried, only he died in his pram instead of his cot. Perfectly well when I put him down.

They do say time heals but believe me, Anne, you never forget. My Robert would have been fifty now. I always have a little weep when I go to his grave. I am nearly seventy-seven years old.

All good wishes to you and Mike and your sons.

Sincerely yours,

Betty Davies
Andover
Hants

In one way, we had to admire the appalling cheek and steely nerve of the man running the *Sun*. Its editor, Kelvin MacKenzie, was a legend in Fleet Street – though not a pleasant one. His name was spoken in soft tones, not out of any reverence, but because everyone was frightened of him.

He it was who was responsible for headlines like 'Gotcha!' when British forces sank the Argentinian ship, the *Belgrano*, during the Falklands war, or 'Freddie Starr Ate My Hamster!' He's the man who printed a picture of a skull all over his front page, claiming it belonged to the man Leslie Grantham murdered. And he's the editor who approved the victimization of Elton John, only to be forced ultimately into paying the superstar a million pounds in damages.

He boldly went, bearing a large, red and not always justified 'exclusive' banner, where other editors feared to tread. On top of that, he had, and enjoyed using, a vocabulary which would make a dockyard navvy blush.

Now, after betraying us at our most vulnerable time, he rang to ask us to a friendly breakfast meeting – to discuss setting up a fund-raising campaign for research into cot death.

The message we received from his office was short and clear: they had had an enormous public reaction to the front page. They wanted to start a *Sun* campaign. Last time they raised money, they had amassed hundreds of thousands of pounds within a very short time. And, again – the old, very effective threat: 'We will do this without you but it will be more effective if you endorse it. But, make no mistake, we will do it anyway without your help.' In legal circles they call it blackmail. In Fleet Street, it's everyday business.

We balked at the thought of being manipulated in this way. But on the other hand, we liked the idea of raising money for research. Through our letters, we were just becoming aware of the magnitude of human suffering caused by this killer known as Sudden Infant Death Syndrome. We still wanted to know what had killed our baby. And if this was the only way to push things forward ... We reluctantly agreed to meet Kelvin MacKenzie, along with one of his lieutenants, Neil Wallis.

We met at a West End hotel for breakfast – though I don't think anyone ate. We sensed that Kelvin was one of those pressmen who likes to keep a distance between himself and the people he preys upon. It's very easy to victimize, to tear a reputation to ribbons, to lambast and lampoon when you don't know the person you are destroying. But once you see the whites of their eyes and realize that they're a fellow human being, it takes a lot more courage.

We both felt that Kelvin seemed a little awkward. He got down to business quickly. 'The *Sun* doesn't do fund-raising,' he said brusquely. 'In fact, it's only ever done it once before in its entire history. But, when it does it, it does it well. And, having the biggest circulation in the country, it raises one hell of a lot of money.'

'How much?' we wanted to know.

'Well, last time it was well over half a million,' he said.

We sat back, and drank our coffee. I tried in vain to hide my shaking hand.

'Last time we did it, it was at the time that they were phasing out the halfpenny, so we appealed for everyone's halfpenny pieces. People in the East End called it the tiddler – so we called the campaign 'Save a Tiddler for a Toddler – and it worked. Instead of giving them in at the bank, they sent them to the *Sun*.'

He leaned forward, across the crisp damask tablecloth, where his coffee spoon had dripped a large puddle of coffee. He nearly put his elbow in it. 'So we thought we could do another Tiddler campaign. It will work again, because everyone hates these little coins...'

He held up a tiny 5p coin. They were becoming well-known as a nuisance, too small for their value – and too easy to lose. 'Well, we can do the same thing all over again. This time it will be for cot death. And we want you to give it your name. Bear in mind, we'll do it without your help. But I think it would work even better if you endorsed it.'

It was almost impossible for us to refuse. We weighed up the conflicting advantages and disadvantages. Some people might not wish to support a campaign which was so closely identified with a down-market newspaper. It might attract criticism from the others, too. But there were a great many *Sun* readers – some twelve million – and they were the very sort of people who could be highly motivated by an emotional issue, particularly one concerning children. Aesthetically, we might have preferred to run a campaign in the *Daily Telegraph* or the *Sunday Times* – but it wouldn't reach as many people.

We agreed. But first there was a rather sticky matter to sort out. We were still deeply in litigation with the *Sun*, over their publication of the interview with our nanny, Debbie, four years before. No way were we just going to abandon our legal case against them. Kelvin dug his heels in, too. No way was the *Sun* going to say sorry and admit its culpability.

But, out of respect for Supi, both sides conceded that there had to be a compromise. We all agreed that the terms of settlement would be private and confidential, but that the *Sun* would pay £10,000 into the new charity, to kick it off. And that this sum would be described as a donation given jointly by the *Sun* and us.

It just shows that disputes, no matter how bitter, can be resolved if the willingness is there. On this occasion, even the hardest man in Fleet Street saw the greater objective.

Mike became engrossed in long discussions with lawyers and accountants from both sides about the setting up of the charity. In fact, it involved reviving the old 'Tiddler' charity and changing its directors, one of whom was Michael Heseltine, the Tory MP and cabinet minister. This all had to be done in consultation with the Charity Commissioners. I, meanwhile, wrote a short piece for publication in the *Sun*, to launch the appeal. It was the first time, too, that Supi's picture would be publicized. I had read so much about his death in the newspapers of the past few days – but no-one had asked for a picture of him. Now I thought it was about time I showed the world how beautiful he was.

When we handed the photos to Neil Wallis, he looked at them long and hard – and then gulped. He told us that he, too, had known the anguish of watching a child fight for life. His baby daughter had spent weeks in an incubator, and had nearly died. He looked again at the snaps of Supi in his bouncy chair, Supi with his brothers the day he was allowed out of Skiboo, Supi with Mike, enjoying a laugh, and Supi with me underneath the vines at the Bunch of Grapes. 'Christ,' he sighed at us. 'You two have got balls.'

My piece was headlined 'Why Did My Baby Die? – Anne Diamond Launches a Fund for You to Give Just a Tiddler to Save a Toddler Like Her Sebastian.' Again, it took up the whole front page. In it, I wrote:

At ten minutes to eight on Friday morning, July 12, I found our little boy Sebastian dead in his cot. He was four months old.

My family are still in deep shock. I don't think I can yet believe it. The coroner later told my husband Mike and myself that Sebastian had died from Sudden Infant Death Syndrome – or cot death.

What no-one has been able to tell us – either then or now – is why he died. We keep asking why and we are told to stop torturing ourselves with the question. But surely it's the only question we should be asking – again and again, until some-one finds out the answer.

We now know that four other babies in Britain died from cot death on the same day we lost Sebastian. I bet those four sets of parents are also asking 'WHY?' just like us.'

Inside – the bold strap: 'Help Us End the Evil of Cot Deaths', and those happy family snaps.

'Weeks after these pictures were taken, this happy group was torn apart when laughing little baby Sebastian died from cot death syndrome,' wrote Neil in his editorial:

'Four other families, all of whom probably have similar happy snaps, were devastated when exactly the same thing happened to them that day.

All are victims of an appalling syndrome that kills 2,000 such lovely, laughing babies a year.

It has got to be stopped. Which is why these pictures are on loan to the *Sun* from Anne and Mike's private family album.

And which is why Anne and the *Sun* today launch the Diamond Cot Death Appeal with a joint £10,000 donation.

Now we are asking you to match that with just one tiny 5p piece.

If every one of our caring family of twelve million *Sun* readers contributed just one 5p coin, it would raise £600,000.'

Readers were asked to organize office collections, start swear boxes, do sponsored events – all for 5p coins.

'Is it worth it?' Neil ended.

'Does it matter? Can your little 5p coin really make any difference?

Look at those pictures again. As Anne and her husband Mike promise you from the bottom of their broken hearts – the answer is yes.'

As I read the words, before they went to print (that was part of the deal), I knew that it was brash, tabloid, sensational journalism. It was written in 'Sunspeak'. I also knew it would work. And they had promised to back up their coverage with a helpline phone number. I strongly believe that if the media creates a scare – and there was no doubt that we were airing a subject which was, however justifiably, bound to cause mass fright, then you had to address that reaction. At the very least we could provide counsellors at the end of a phone line.

The money started rolling in from that day. The paper did constant updates. One day, they held a telephone auction. Stars such as George Michael and Elton John donated items for inclusion. On that day alone, we raised £35,000.

Sebastian was beginning to make his mark. But I still had no idea of how immense and far-reaching that mark was to be.

Chapter 15

We needed to get away – so Mike, me, Shirley, and the boys went back to the hotel in the Lake District where we had spent a few glorious, yet rainy and windswept, days with Supi. It was, maybe, a sort of pilgrimage for Mike, since his childhood friend, John Chapman, lived there. I already had the love and support of my best friend, Shirley. He needed to talk, too, to a friend he'd known and trusted since schooldays. When you are bereaved, you can tolerate no pretence. You need the sort of love that is understood – because you are already vulnerable. John and his wife, Sue, sat and listened to us for hours.

They were a lovely couple, with two grown daughters, both of whom would undoubtedly leave home within a few years. John and Sue spoke of their plans to buy a house with enough land to keep horses. Sue was excited. It was something she had always wanted to do. It was the first time I had met them both, and I liked them immediately.

But in Carlisle I first experienced a feeling of loss which was to haunt me for months. Mike and I, Shirley and the two boys, were shopping in the central pedestrian precinct. We had been there just a matter of months before and I had popped into the various baby shops to buy a baby-carrier for Supi. Now, all I could see were babies in buggies. Little, laughing, gurgling babies being pushed towards me, past me, away from me. Every time I saw a pair of chubby little legs in a buggy, I scanned the baby's face to see if it was Supi. If a buggy went past before I could see the child's face, I found my eyes following it, my legs almost chasing it, until I could satisfy myself that it wasn't him. When we were driving along in the car, my eyes would fix upon every pushchair in the street. And then I would realize what I was doing, and break down.

Why was I searching for him? I knew he was dead – I'd seen his body. And yet I felt an obsessive urge, a compulsion, to just make sure he wasn't in that stroller, or in that one...I was bewildered. Was I going mad? Was I one step away from taking someone's else's baby? Was this what turned ordinary women into baby snatchers?

Yet I didn't want anyone else's baby – I only wanted mine. I wanted him so much that my arms ached. My breasts, even though we had long abandoned the breastfeeding, almost burned with the desire to feed him. I could hear his chuckle around every corner. I could see his little legs kicking their socks off in every buggy around me. And the disappointment, when I found that the face wasn't his, was driving me insane. In the middle of the busy precinct, I just stopped and tears started streaming down my cheeks. Mike, Shirley and the boys clasped themselves around me in one big human pyramid.

We must have seemed a strange sight, but no-one commented. If they recognized us, they probably understood. The tenderness of many strangers was very comforting. After we had popped into town once for some errand, a London cabbie had refused to take his fare. We hadn't even exchanged words – but he instantly recognized us. 'I couldn't take anything off you, mate, not after what you've been through,' he said to Mike. 'I've got kids, too. Put it towards your cot death fund...'

While total strangers often knew how to handle us, some friends and acquaintances would cross the street rather than meet us face to face. One old colleague from Central TV saw us coming towards him in the middle of a shop. I could see his eyes dart around for an escape route. But he couldn't avoid us. Instead he bounced up, thrust his hands into his raincoat pockets and said the first thing that came into his head – something

I knew he would rather have not said: 'Hi! Long time no see! So... how's life?' We could see that he wanted a trapdoor to open up and swallow him.

Down at the Catholic church, we were swamped with well-meaning hugs, hand-clasps and slappings on the back. 'The next one will be a girl,' so many of them said. Or: 'You've got a little angel in Heaven.' I lit my candles – but I didn't really have faith that anyone up there was watching me. The statue of the Virgin Mary, holding the infant Jesus in her arms, looked down upon me, through her vast pile of floral offerings (still with the Marks & Spencers price-tag on them). How could Christ's mother, with whom I was always told I shared a birthday, allow my son to be taken from me? Surely she knew the pain of such a loss? And yet I still prayed to her. You can erase the Catholic from your head, but never from your heart. I still felt that maybe if I prayed hard enough she could bring Supi back to me.

I prayed and prayed into the night as I lay in bed next to a sleeping Mike. Occasionally he awoke to find my face wet with tears, and me unglamorously blowing my nose to cover up. He would comfort me – but he thought I was simply mourning my son. I wasn't. I was praying so damned hard that I thought my brain would explode. If miracles can happen, then I want one now, I demanded silently of God. I'll be the first mother in the whole history of mankind who will simply refuse to accept a child's death. I won't tolerate what fate has doled out to me – I simply won't have it.

I prayed and prayed. I'll test them, I thought. If God and his Son can work miracles, then let's see them do it. But in the morning, nothing had changed.

Following our visit to John and Sue Chapman, we travelled back down the motorway from Carlisle to London on the day that John McCarthy, British hostage in Beirut, was released. It was wonderful news. But I kept thinking – Jill Morrell, the girl-friend who fought so hard for his release, has had the answer

145

to her prayers. I'll never get mine. And I felt ashamed for begrudging her such joy.

Two days after we'd returned home, and while we were having a quiet Sunday morning with Oliver and Jamie, Mike received a phone call from Sue in Carlisle. It was shocking news. John was dead. He'd been walking the dog early that morning, and had simply dropped down dead on the pavement. It was a massive heart attack. And so, within days of organizing his own son's funeral, Mike found himself attending the funeral of his best friend. Hundreds of people turned out for the service. John was a very popular man, a church usher and a member of the local rugby club.

Sue and I rushed into each other's arms. I barely knew her, but I knew her pain. John's funeral was a large affair – a demonstration of feeling from everyone who had known him. Supi's funeral had been tiny in comparison – but the emotion as strong. It made me realize that, in human terms, the only real difference between the two people we had just lost was the size of their coffins. Because although Supi had lived just four and a half months (plus another eight months inside me) his effect on those who knew him was just as strong as if he'd lived fifty years.

Several people, notably those who didn't have children, remarked to me: 'Aren't you lucky you didn't really have time to get to know your son? He was with you such a short time.' It was an agonizingly insensitive thing to say – though clearly a great many people think it, when someone loses a baby. But what they'd never understand is that our child was with us for a whole lifetime. The moment we knew of his existence, he became part of the plot which was our family story. He was immediately built into the computer programme which mapped out the rest of our lives. At six months, he was going to sit up. At nine, to crawl. From now on, we'd need a house with an extra bedroom. And more money for school fees. Another seat on the airliner for holidays. Would he want to go to university? Would I like his girlfriends?

146

We hadn't just lost a baby of four and a half months. We'd lost a schoolboy, a teenager, a pimply adolescent, a college student, a young man, a father with children of his own – our grandchildren. And there was nothing in that computer programme which allowed for his sudden cancellation. I was still the mother of a four-month-old baby boy. All the maternal instincts, the inbuilt reactions, even the way I was physically (still overweight, but hardly caring), were part of a programme which had been dramatically interrupted. No wonder I was feeling wretched. And it was while I was almost drowning in a quagmire of hopelessness that Mike took a call from a woman named Linda McDougall.

'Who's she?'

'Well,' said Mike, who knew her but only vaguely. 'She's quite well-known as a film producer and documentary maker. Used to work on *The Cook Report* and such like. She's also the wife of the Labour MP Austin Mitchell. '

'What does she want?'

'Well, that's just it... she wouldn't say. Very secretive. She wants to meet for lunch. And she particularly doesn't want you there...'

He came back from the lunch strangely excited, and almost scared to tell me what he'd heard.

'She's from New Zealand,' he started.

Yes, yes, I thought. Very nice to hear about her birthright. But what did she have to say?

'Well, she really wants to tell you all about it herself. It's to do with cot death. It seems they're experts on it in New Zealand – and they might have found an answer.'

So I agreed to meet Linda, too. She had approached Mike first, because she was afraid I might be too upset to handle what she had to tell us. I have to say that this was the first and last time I have ever known Linda be sensitive to anyone's feelings, particularly mine. I met her at a small restaurant in Hammersmith, near the hospital, and opposite LBC, the capital's talk radio station, where I had been standing in for Michael Parkinson on his morning show. Mike had thought it would be a good way to gradually rehabilitate me to everyday life.

Linda was a remarkable woman, I could tell that from the moment she started to speak. She was about forty, medium build, and with a stack of blonde, short hair. She looked the part – a shrewd, hard-nosed journalist – more interested in 'the story' than the glamour of TV. She was probably the sort of producer who usually looked down with contempt upon people like me, who become 'celebrities'.

It's difficult to find words to describe Linda that won't immediately invite a writ. To say she is brusque would be a serious understatement. She would consider it her duty to truth and honour to call a spade a bloody shovel, and to expose bullshit at any cost. To say she was cold would be to deny the humanity which motivated her journalistic instinct. She was, as the Americans would say, a tough cookie, who sometimes forgot to be pleasant. Today, though, she was as gentle as a lamb. But she delivered a punch.

'My old mum regularly sends me newspapers from New Zealand, so I can keep up with home news,' she started. 'And in one of them, I read a remarkable thing...' She leaned forward, and stared me in the eyes. 'The Kiwis have been doing a huge campaign against cot death. Did you know anything at all about this?'

I shook my head, eager to hear more.

'Well, apparently they've found a way to prevent it. And they've had incredible success. It's something to do with the way babies sleep – and overheating, and smoking. But they've been telling mothers in New Zealand to do certain things – and it works.'

I had that feeling again, of my heart wanting to explode out of my chest. I could feel its beat thumping through my rib-cage. Like the morning I'd discovered Supi dead.

'What position did your baby sleep in?' she asked me

bluntly. It was the second time I'd been asked that question.

'On his tummy,' I replied. 'That's the way you're meant to do it – it's better for them.'

'No, it isn't,' said Linda, ominously. 'Apparently that's what's killing them. Or, rather,' she corrected herself, 'that is what is making them *susceptible* to cot death.'

I sat for a moment, trying to take in what she'd just said. And then came a thousand questions.

'Look, I don't know the answers to any of this,' Linda said. And then she threw her arms upwards. 'But don't you think someone should be asking those questions for all the other mums out there who don't want their baby to die like Anne Diamond's?'

I knew immediately what she meant. We journalists needed to ask what was going on. We needed to go to New Zealand and find out what they had discovered. *Was there really a cure for cot death? What was it? And why didn't we know about it in this country?*

And then, a question which seared through me like a lance: *Could I have saved Supi?*

Chapter 16

And so we found ourselves, one cold, rainy morning, 12,000 miles away from home, on a dank, miserable beach in North Island, New Zealand.

'This is one of our greatest tourist attractions,' said Linda, disappointed. 'This is Waihi beach. It's usually bristling with people surfing and barbecueing. I'm afraid I'm not going to get the shots I really wanted with this weather...'

This was the first day of filming – and Linda had even rented a beach house so that we could shelter from the sun in between takes. But it was October – and this was an example of a damp Kiwi spring day. Shirley, Alex and the boys were with me. We were only eight weeks from Supi's death, and still very raw. I couldn't leave the children behind, half way across the world. So I had brought them along. Besides, if we were going to find out what killed Supi – then it was a crusade which involved the whole family. Oliver already understood that much, and had told his friends at nursery school that he was going to find out why his baby brother had died.

Mike had commitments, and couldn't come straight away. Unbelievably, another friend of his was close to death. Alan, a highly respected TV producer and director (he directed the notorious BBC Royal *It's A Knockout!*), had cancer. Since the diagnosis at around Supi's birthday, Alan's health had rapidly deteriorated. Mike, so practical in crisis, was doing everything possible to support Alan and his girlfriend, Karen.

Many, many evenings, we had debated long and hard with Karen whether Alan should continue with traditional treatments, or try a less orthodox dietary approach. Mike had helped get them a Macmillan nurse. But now Alan was in hospital – literally on his deathbed. And it was Mike who helped the couple achieve their dearest wish – to get married.

'I can't leave Alan now,' Mike had said to me, just days before we were to fly to New Zealand. 'I don't think he has many days left. I want to be here for Karen.'

I understood. But Mike was worried about how I would cope with the fearsome Linda McDougall, without protection. We were anxious that this documentary should remain tightly controlled, as we were inevitably going to expose our grief on TV. We knew that, as well as investigating the medical angle, we would have to tell our own personal story. But the Revd Fred Rason's words rang in our ears: *What you do now, you will have to live with for the rest of your lives.* So Shirley was recruited as my bodyguard – with strict instructions to keep an eye on Linda.

But things went wrong almost immediately. As soon as we had arrived, limp as wet lettuces from the twenty-six-hour flight to Auckland, I was called to a meeting with Linda, and the co-producer, Jan Euden. 'The story has changed quite considerably from what we thought it was going to be,' they announced to me.

What was that? The hackles on the back of my neck started to rise. 'What do you mean?'

'Well,' said Jan, who had spent the last three weeks researching all the major medics on the New Zealand cot death scene, 'this is no longer about what causes cot death. It's no longer about the mechanics of death – because they still don't know that.'

But that's what I'd come all this way to discover, wasn't it?

'What they've found, is a way to reduce the risks of cot death.'

It didn't sound madly exciting to me. I wanted to know what cot death *was.* I'd read so much about it by now. There were theories that the baby stops breathing because it is in too deep a sleep. I had heard ideas that it might be due to stress – that we left our babies alone in cots for too long, almost in a state of sensory deprivation, with empty stomachs because we expected them to sleep through the night, without constant feeding. I had felt guilty about that one, though I clung to the fact that according to the pathologist's report there was still milk inside Supi's stomach when he died. So he hadn't been hungry.

What about the theory that it might be an allergy to cows' milk? Or biological washing powder? Or a reaction to electrical fields, or even ley-lines? Those were the theories I was anxious to investigate. Now Linda and Jan were going on about something called risk reduction... What on earth was that?

Over the next few days, I began to learn that this thing called 'risk reduction' was what was going to save hundreds and thousands of babies. And not just New Zealanders, but *our* babies. *British* babies. And Australian babies, and Tasmanian babies, and Dutch babies, and French babies, and Belgian babies, and Irish babies, and German babies and Canadian babies, and American babies. In fact, it was going to save the lives of babies wherever it was tried.

So we waited on windy Waihi beach for my first interviewee. 'You'll really love her,' promised Linda. 'She's Mrs Cot Death of New Zealand. There isn't anything about cot death which she doesn't know.'

Shirley Tonkin blew on to that beach like the strong force she was known to be in her country. Small – only about five feet – petite and mousy, you would never guess that this was a woman who had dedicated her life to the study of children, and whose work would have world-wide consequences. She was a paediatrician – and had become increasingly concerned over the years at the number of cot deaths she had witnessed. In fact, New Zealand had the highest cot death rate in the world, and no-one knew why.

Linda took me to one side and whispered gleefully in my

ear: 'She's also the mother of Heather Tonkin – Bonkin Tonkin, the girl who had the affair with Captain Mark Phillips!'

Up and down the beach I strolled with Shirley Tonkin, while Linda and her cameraman searched for the right shots. Mrs Tonkin had been told my history – she knew all about Supi – and she was worried for me: 'You know you shouldn't be here,' she said to me, quite sternly. 'You should be at home. Are you sure you want to do this?'

I told her about my anguish at seeing other people's babies – and how I looked for Supi in every pram.

'That's because you haven't accepted his death yet,' she said. 'You're still searching for him. '

We must have walked miles, trudging up and down that soggy beach, as the soundman recorded our conversation. I told Shirley Tonkin how I had found Supi, on his tummy, up against the bars of the cot. I mentioned the little dent on his head, where he'd pushed himself against the bars.

'That's exactly how we're finding a lot of these babies,' she said. 'So many of them have wriggled into a corner and then got themselves wedged into a position they cannot get out of.'

She looked at me again, concerned. 'Are you sure you're going to be all right doing this documentary?' she asked. 'I think you should be at home with your husband, and starting the long process of learning to live with your grief. You cannot avoid it, you know.'

I did know. But even stronger than my grief right now was a feeling of vengeance. I wanted to avenge my son's death. I wanted to kill what had killed him. Only then could I embrace the grim luxury of mourning.

We were deep in conversation, and I was warming greatly to this small woman with the big heart, when Linda came bounding up to us. 'That's great!' she said. 'Now I just want you to go down to the far end of the beach again, and walk through that rainbow...' A huge arc of coloured light had formed in the

154

distance. It seemed to be growing out of the wet sand at the water's edge. Linda saw a shot worth having – and we duly trudged down to the rainbow's end.

When we'd finished with the visual poetry, we were cold and windswept. I needed to talk with Linda about our return tickets, which she was supposedly organizing. I had only a very short window in my diary to shoot the New Zealand footage, because I was due to do *TV Weekly* live the following week. It was imperative I get back to Britain on time, and Linda had promised to arrange the flights. But she hadn't mentioned them yet.

'Linda, I need to make sure those flights are booked.'

'Oh, for God's sake,' she sighed at me. 'How can you go on about flights at a time like this? Can't you see what we're doing here is important?'

'I just need to make sure. If I'm not back in time to do *TV Weekly*...'

This was the wrong way to tackle Linda. The notion that another programme might be as important, or even have priority over hers, was beyond her comprehension.

'*TV Weekly* is my job – I'm under contract to be there to do it,' I sighed. 'And you did say you'd arrange it...'

'Oh, my God,' she sighed again, melodramatically. ' I think you're got the wrong priorities here...You've got totally the wrong attitude to the job!'

At that, I saw red. 'Don't you dare accuse me of having the wrong priorities!' I yelled at her. The camera crew backed away, uncomfortably. They sensed a duel. 'I don't need to be told about priorities! I lost my baby just eight weeks ago – I think I know how important this all is!' And I stormed off.

Looking back, she had been tactless and I oversensitive. But then, I probably had every right to be. Alex, Shirley and the children were inside the beach house, sorting out sandwiches, biscuits and tea. They saw me run off, obviously in distress. Linda stormed in, and up to Alex.

'Does your boss usually go off the deep end at the slightest word?' she spat.

My bodyguard, Shirley, came after me.

'So help me, I cannot stand that woman,' I wailed at Shirley. 'She's had us waltzing up and down a bloody beach all day. What's she doing? Making a travel film?'

Shirley put her arm around me. 'Come on, let's go back to the hotel and we'll ring Mike.' But Mike was already on his way to us. Alan, his friend, seemed to be better, and Mike was confident enough to leave Britain. He was expected at Auckland within the next twenty-four hours.

The next day we filmed at Shirley Tonkin's office – and she showed us videos, which she'd recorded with an infra-red camera, of babies as they slept during the night. They were mostly babies of about four months, the 'classic' cot death age. They were put down to sleep on their stomachs, and during the night, while they were still deeply asleep, they wriggled and writhed their way up or down the cot. She was particularly interested in babies with breathing problems, or who had once had breathing problems because they had been premature births. They were high in the cot death statistics. Shirley reckoned that they got themselves in positions in which it would be difficult for them to continue breathing.

'Many of them get stuck in one corner of the cot,' she said. 'And, although they can effectively wriggle one way, they seem to be unable to go into reverse. So they seem to be getting themselves into a fix.'

She said it was particularly worrying where the cots had 'bumpers' or pads along the side of the cot. 'So many babies seem to bury their faces into these bumpers,' she said.

So the ones who had died from cot death – had they in fact suffocated themselves?

'It's difficult to say,' said Shirley Tonkin, shaking her head. The wall behind her was covered with snapshots of babies – many of them babies who had died. 'But one thing started to nag me, as I questioned all the parents after they'd suffered a cot death,' she went on. 'When I asked them to describe how they'd found their baby dead – it started to occur to me that they all started their terrible story using the same words...'

What were they, I asked.

'They all said... *"When I turned the baby over..."* '

Yes? What of it?

'Well – it began to strike me that *all the babies had been on their tummies*. Hardly ever did we seem to get a baby who didn't need turning over for the parents to see its face. By far and away, the babies who were dying from cot death were the babies who were on their tummies.'

Chapter 17

The next day I brushed away my growing disquiet with Linda's attitude. I was eager to get on with the job, and find out more. We were set to go to Auckland's biggest hospital and meet Ed Mitchell, a consultant paediatrician and guardian of the computer files which were processing the world's newest cot death information.

He was a friendly, bearded man. British born and married to an English woman, he had worked in New Zealand for many years, and he had headed New Zealand's cot death study, set up to find out why this little country had the highest cot death rate in the world. It was almost a national scandal. If you were a mum or dad in New Zealand, you had either had a cot death yourself, or you knew someone who had. It was that common.

'We couldn't understand why,' explained Ed. 'New Zealand has one of the best records in the world for child care – and yet we were losing more babies to Sudden Infant Death Syndrome than anyone else...We simply had to find out why. So we all got together and set up the first, and most comprehensive, cot death study in the world.'

When was this, I asked.

'Well, it started in 1988.' Right. I logged the date in my brain. That's three years ago, I thought.

Ed went on: 'It's what we call an epidemiological inquiry. Not a laboratory study or series of experiments – but an investigation into every cot death that occurred.'

So if you were the parents of a baby in New Zealand, and you had just found your baby dead, as we had with Supi, you would immediately be visited by Ed Mitchell or one of his

159

team. They were trained in handling newly bereaved parents, but also wise to the fact that most parents were keen to co-operate. They wanted to know what had killed their baby.

You would be asked about everything that could conceivably be relevant. Boy or girl? How old? Breastfed or bottle-fed? Brothers and sisters?

Was your baby unwell in any way? Had he behaved any differently from normal? Was he 'himself' that day? Had you recently changed his routine?

Had he been immunized? Recent coughs and colds or viral illnesses? Did he suck a dummy? Did his parents smoke? Or drink? All these questions, and hundreds more, had to be agreed as part of the 'protocol' of the investigation, so that direct comparisons could later be made.

'And we built into the protocol some questions about sleep position,' said Ed. 'Because the theory about sleep position had been circulating in medical circles for some time – though the whole world pooh-poohed it. We built it into our questionnaire so that we could successfully prove it one way or the other.' Other factors, too, were built into the protocol for the study, which was designed to continue for three years.

Then, as one expert was asking these questions of you, another member of Mitchell's team would find two more families living in the same neighbourhood, with a child of the same age, and ask exactly the same questions of them. These were called 'control' cases. By comparing the data of the dead children and their 'controls', the computer could start to build up a picture. Effectively, it might then tell you why one baby had died that night, and two others had not.

'And what did the computer say?' I asked.

'Well, at first we were just logging the information in,' explained Ed. 'It was some eighteen months before reliable data started coming *out*. But when it did, we were staggered. The babies who were dying were generally the ones who slept on their tummies.'

I was numb. Ed Mitchell took me by the arm. 'Are you all right?' he asked. 'Maybe you shouldn't be doing this. You can't run away from your own grief – this is bound to be hitting you hard.' I made him go on. 'Well,' he continued. 'We found that we were also losing babies who were put down to sleep on their backs or sides. *But when they were found dead, they were on their stomachs.* They had rolled over in the night.'

Ed explained that this discovery threw the doctors and the scientists into turmoil – and conflict. The doctors thought it would be immoral to continue the study without telling New Zealand's mothers what they had found. They felt sure that they could save lives if they told mothers to avoid sleeping their babies on their stomachs. The scientists, proud and excited by the data, insisted that the three-year study must go on for the full three years. To interfere with the way mothers treated their children throughout the country would ruin the data they had already amassed.

'Morally, we could do nothing else but tell the mothers,' said Ed. 'We knew that doing so might ruin other, and possibly more vital, data. But we had to give mothers a chance to save their babies' lives.' So the cot death experts got together and agreed that they should actively campaign with the new message – turn your baby over.

'You can see how difficult it was,' said Ed. 'We didn't really know what we were advising – or the effect it would have. We had no idea at all why it might save a baby from cot death. We just knew we had to try.'

So, looking at all the research data emerging from the first eighteen months of their study, they figured out the main areas of advice. Seventy-three per cent of the cot death babies had been lying on their stomachs, sixty-three per cent had mothers who smoked and over a third were not being breastfed. If the child was lying on his stomach, was not breastfed and had a mother who smoked, he was ten times more likely to die from cot death.

This needed a mass media campaign. Shirley Tonkin knew that there was only one way to reach a large number of people quickly, efficiently and dramatically. Television. She was adamant that they must make an advert to be shown on TV, so she recruited the best known female news presenter in New Zealand to present a thirty-second message, telling mums to lie their babies on their backs or sides.

In New Zealand, it was huge news. Within days, there wasn't a parent, grandparent or babysitter who didn't know the new advice.

1. Lie your baby on his back or side to sleep. If you lie him on his side, make sure that the underneath arm is well forward, to stop the baby rolling on to his stomach.

2. Don't smoke.

3. Breastfeed if you possibly can.

'We put everything we could into the message,' said Ed, as he flashed through the computer graphs which backed up the advice.

And Shirley Tonkin took up the story: she knew it was a message that must reach not just mothers but every member of the family. 'It's not just mum who looks after the baby in any household,' she said. 'There are brothers and sisters, grandmas and grandpas – even the girl next door who does the babysitting. We had to reach them all. There's only one way to do that – TV. We didn't just want prime-time advertising, we needed to put out the ad in the middle of the daytime soaps and quiz shows.'

They even borrowed the British idea of a Red Nose Day – not for Comic Relief as in Britain, but for cot death awareness. Politicians of both parties joined together, red noses touching, to proclaim the news that New Zealand had found an answer to cot death.

I was breathless just to hear the story. 'And what happened?' I asked.

'Our cot death rate fell by fifty per cent within six months,' said Ed, matter-of-factly, but with the hint of a smile under his moustache.

And *when* did this all happen, I urged.

'Almost a year ago,' he replied.

So while this had all been going on, at the other end of our planet, I had been happily putting my baby to sleep on his stomach, safe in the knowledge – or so I thought – that it was the best thing to do. I hesitated, and then asked almost in a whisper: 'Why didn't you tell anyone in Britain?'

Ed shook his head sadly, knowing that what he was to say would hurt me badly. 'Everyone knows about what we're doing. We told your government about it, and the Foundation for the Study of Infant Deaths in your country has even funded part of it. We *did* tell Britain. We *did*. I don't know why they didn't do anything.'

Chapter 18

Who could go to New Zealand with two little boys and not pop along to the All Blacks shop to buy them mini-versions of the full rugby strip? Oliver and Jamie were enjoying their trip – they didn't see much of their mummy, but I felt that at least we were all together at night, when I was at my most fearful.

As soon as Mike joined me, he took me to meet a friend of his, who was now the Director General of New Zealand Television, a man called Julian Mounter. Mike knew that Julian Mounter had once worked with Linda McDougall. We were now so anxious about her that we decided to ask Julian his advice. He met us in his glass-walled office on top of a hill overlooking the city of Auckland. And while we drank coffee and munched biscuits, he told us what he thought.

'I'm not in the least surprised you're finding it hard going with her,' he said, his eyebrows laughing. 'She is well-known for it. But, frankly, she's a bloody good journalist and I don't think she's ever turned in a bad film.'

So we decided to grimace and bear it, and go on with the next stage of our filming schedule. Alex, Shirley, Mike and the boys were to fly to Christchurch. Meanwhile Linda, Jan, the camera crew and I were to do the same journey by car, but also visit Dunedin, Linda's home town, where she'd met Austin, her husband. At the university, a doctor called Barry Richards was researching the effects of overheating on babies. They were experimenting in their laboratories with piglets, warming their bodies very slightly, to see what effects this had on their sleeping physiology.

One theory they were investigating was the thought that, under certain stressful conditions, babies exercised a primitive instinct to 'shut down' their systems. There were stories of how, in the Mexico earthquake and other disasters, babies had been rescued alive and well for up to ten days afterwards, though they had had no food, nor even water. Some cot death experts reckoned that babies who died from cot death had inadvertently – maybe because of being too hot – set this 'shut down' reflex into action, but had been unable to bring themselves back to consciousness. But this still didn't explain why New Zealand should have the highest cot death rate in the world. And why should there be more deaths in the South Island than the North?

'It may be because it gets so cold down here,' said Barry. 'Mothers look at the cold weather outside and wrap their babies accordingly, forgetting that they're indoors in a heated house. We've tried wrapping our piglets in the same clothes and covers that a typical Dunedin mum would use – and it's sent the piglets into distress. Now we're telling mums to clothe and wrap their babies in exactly the same amount of layers that they themselves would be comfortable in. We're also telling them to put away those sheepskins. They may be doing more harm than good.'

In the evening, we visited one of the mothers under his care – a girl, Penny Gray, who had already lost one child. Her new baby was now at the vulnerable age – four months. She showed me how she put her to bed under the new guidelines. 'On her back, and near the bottom of the Moses basket so she can't wriggle down any further under the blankets,' she recited, as though she had learned it by heart. 'And we don't use cot bumpers or duvets, just old-fashioned sheets and blankets.'

Then she put a breathing monitor on an elastic strap around her chest – and a green light blipped every time she took a breath.

'Sometimes the alarm goes off in the middle of the night,

and we nearly have a heart attack,' she said. 'And we log every time that it goes off, so that we talk it over with the doctor next time we see him. Because if it goes off too many times, either we're doing something wrong, or she's having trouble with her breathing.'

She looked at me, and I could see that she was being brave for us, for the camera. 'So far, so good,' she sighed. Cot death was almost an expected hazard in her family. She'd lost her own daughter, her husband had lost a brother and they had both lost cousins to cot death. At the family funeral of their daughter, Christie, there had been fifteen families who had lost a baby to cot death. With four or five babies dying in every thousand (with a population of only three million), it was hardly surprising that cot death had touched nearly everyone in New Zealand.

But the little girl I met the next morning was hardly out of childhood herself before she was plunged into the loss and bereavement of her own baby. We had stayed overnight in a motel in Dunedin – and the crew, Jan, Linda and I ate breakfast as we decided on the best route up to Christchurch. Linda was engrossed in the local paper. I looked to see what was engaging her – and noticed that she was scanning the classified adverts section, and particularly the Births, Marriages and Deaths.

'I'm looking to see if there's been a cot death recently,' she said. 'Of course, it's relatively rare nowadays, but you never know...'

We went on eating our toast and butter. Full cream butter, and full cream milk in the tea. Every meal in New Zealand seemed to be oozing with dairy products, and bathing in a sea of cholesterol.

'Aha! This looks like one...' And she read out:

> BIDDLE, baby Jesse Rangiora, Mihaere. On October 1, 1991 (suddenly at his home)

treasured son of Cecilia and Shane, much
loved grandson of Moana Biddle and Robyn
Wilson, and his many relatives and friends;
aged three and a half months.

'Right. I'm going to phone them.'

The cameraman and I looked at each other in disbelief.
Surely Linda wasn't going to barge in on a family which had
just suffered a cot death? Surely she didn't intend for us to go
and film them? Surely she didn't expect me to go?

She bounded back, enthusiastically. 'Yep, it is a cot death.
The child died yesterday. They're a Maori family, so the baby
is still with them, with the relatives all around. Come on, I
think I know where it is. Let's get going.' She turned to me.
'Do you want to come? I shall understand if you don't...'

I didn't know what to say, or what to think. 'Yes, I'll come.
But I might stay in the car.'

We drove uphill, and turned into a housing estate. At the
end of a small cul-de-sac was our destination, a cheap, tatty
house built in the sixties with shoddy materials which hadn't
stood the test of time.

'Linda,' I asked, still uncertain that I wanted to go in. 'How
did the baby die, do we know?'

Linda shook her head. 'The family elder who I spoke to said
that the baby had been in bed with his grandmother. It's not
clear exactly what position he'd been in, or anything.' She
turned to the crew. 'Right, we all need to make a gift,' she said
brightly. 'When you enter a Maori house, you have to take a
small offering – usually silver coins. It's a tradition which I
think we should respect since they're allowing us in...'

We all felt in our pockets for loose change. Jan put it all into
an envelope, and they went forward to the front door. Linda
looked back at me.

'I'll come,' I said, and brought up the rear.

The family elder opened the door. He was a huge man, tall

and round, dressed in shabby old clothes and still wearing slippers. He accepted our gift, and led us in. His face was hang-dog with melancholy. We were shown into a large room, bare except for mattresses on the floor. There were no curtains, only a couple of white sheets stretched over the window, and someone had sellotaped six or seven family photos on to them, so that they were silhouetted against the light.

On the floor, sitting dejectedly on one of the mattresses was a young Maori girl. She looked all of fifteen. The skin on her face was blotched with pink and purple patches, and her eyes looked as though they had been crying for ever. And next to her, like a tiny china doll, was her baby boy. He was lying on his back, with his arms crossed in front, wearing a knitted cardigan and bonnet, and his tiny body wrapped in a shawl. His little eyes were tight shut and his delicate mouth pursed, almost in a Cupid's-bow kiss. He was dead.

There were 12,000 miles, an entire culture and at least twenty years between this young mother and myself – but I had more in common with her at that moment than anyone else in that room. I walked over to her instinctively, knelt down on the mattress, and clutched her hand.

'I'm so sorry. I lost my baby, too, just eight weeks ago. I know how you feel. I'm so terribly sorry.' And then I looked down at her dead child, and stroked his little cheek. I recognized that deep, chilling cold of dead flesh.

And I thought of what I had liked to hear people say. 'Poor little mite. He is beautiful, absolutely beautiful.'

Various of her relatives were making cups of tea. Others were visiting because they'd just heard the news, or read the notice in the paper. A Maori baby stays within the family for three days after death, because they believe the spirit can still be there for that time. The family elder started praying aloud, and chanting. He cannot have been a very close relative, we thought, because he kept getting the sex of the baby wrong. It was a boy, and yet he kept saying prayers for 'her' and 'her short life'.

We thought we should leave. The crew shuffled out, and I followed. Linda came up to me with a bunch of flowers which she'd bought at the motel. 'I thought you might like to give her these,' she offered. I took them from her, impressed at the kindness of the thought.

I went back in, and saw the young mother now standing in the doorway of the mattress room. We walked towards each other and hugged – and I gave her the flowers. She was starting to cry again. As I closed the front door behind me, and made for the path, I was aware that Linda had the camera trained on my face. She had been trying to film the whole episode.

'Oh my God,' I sighed, and rolled my eyes upwards in despair. At least that would make the shot unusable. I was beginning to have the same respect for her that I had for Kelvin MacKenzie, the editor of the *Sun*. They were both extremely good at their job, but that didn't mean you had to like their tactics.

Maybe Linda prided herself, and still does, on her ability to shock, or surprise you. At any rate, she had her tender moments. She was always lovely to the children – and when the trip was over, she gave me a still-frame from the film, printed as a photo and framed. On the back of the frame, she wrote: 'To Anne – to prove that even nightmares have their good times!' The photograph was of me and Jamie choosing an All Blacks cap, with Oliver looking on. It was a beautiful picture, not the least because it had been carefully composed by an artful director. Later, when the children were buying souvenirs of their New Zealand trip, Jamie bought a big, fluffy penguin and christened it Linda. She was really touched!

At Christchurch airport we met the family so that we could all travel onwards to Queenstown, in the southernmost part of South Island. Queenstown was the country's most beautiful resort – high up in the mountains, it was famous for its ski-ing and snow-sports. This was where Linda wanted her scenic shots for background illustration to the main story of the documentary. So now we could relax a little, and unwind, even though the weather was biting cold. The boys wanted to go and see a sheep station – and there was a touristy one across Lake Wakatipu, where the boys could pat baby lambs and nibble lamb chops for lunch in the restaurant.

On the way back, aboard the steamship *Earnslaw* which spluttered to and fro across the lake all day, we were nearly swamped by a coach-load of Japanese tourists. As soon as they had all ordered their glasses of Coca Cola, they gathered on the main deck and a pianist started belting out an array of sing-along tunes. We had to pinch ourselves to make sure we weren't hallucinating. We were in New Zealand, aboard a steam ferry, with hundreds of Japanese tourists singing 'Roll Out the Barrel' and 'Maybe It's Because I'm a Londoner'.

Then the pianist segued into 'Daisy, Daisy', which was my sons' party piece. Oliver and Jamie stood up, and joined in the singing. At once, the Japanese tourists stopped, and let the little boys sing alone. It was the high point of the whole trip for them. That, and the kiwi-burgers you could get from McDonald's in Queenstown. They were basically a hamburger with a slice of kiwi fruit on the top. Ugh. But the boys liked them.

There was also a large restaurant on the top of a high cliff, which you could only easily reach by ski-lift. The children called it 'the restaurant at the top of the world', because you could see its lights from our hotel rooms, twinkling in the middle of a black sky. After one magical meal there, we walked back through the darkness to the hotel. There, Mike had a message. It was from Karen, telling him that Alan had died peacefully in his sleep. We drank a toast to him, to John and to Supi – and wondered if they had all three reached the same destination.

We returned to Britain via Los Angeles, where we stopped off for two nights to take the boys to Disneyland. I thought we needed to get away from all talk of cot death, away from hospitals and research laboratories. And away from Linda and her crew. I hadn't seen very much of the boys during the fortnight we were away, except at night, and I wanted to be with them. But while we were sitting in an open-air restaurant at the end of Mainstreet USA, in the 'Magic Kingdom' of Mickey Mouse, busily chomping into the most enormous hot-dogs, Oliver looked up quizzically.

'Daddy,' he started... 'What is cot death? Did we find out?'

'No,' said Mike, truthfully. 'No, we didn't find out exactly. But we did find a way to prevent it happening to other babies.'

'So what are we going to do now?'

'We're going to go home and find out why we didn't know about it sooner, that's what.'

And that is exactly what we did. The moment we set foot again on British soil, we would start lobbying in every way we knew possible. We would thump on the front door of the Department of Health so loud they couldn't fail to hear the din. *'Look again at the evidence you have so negligently ignored,'* we would rail at them, until they were sick of us. *'Then tell us why it cannot save British babies, too.'*

Chapter 19

I only just made it home on time. I had flown alone on Virgin Airways from Los Angeles to Heathrow, and then caught a light plane from London to Southampton in order to be in the TVS studios with enough time to rehearse, and to make the usual live transmission of *TV Weekly*.

Chris Riley, head of the team, knew why I'd been to New Zealand, and must have realized that I was very preoccupied during those days – but instead of being annoyed by this, the whole team did all they could to make life a little easier for me. After all, they had known Supi. They had all met him when he was just four weeks old. After that first broadcast, just days after I had given birth and I had had to leave Supi behind in Skiboo, I had always taken him to work with me, and he had been looked after in my dressing room by Nanny Anne.

Now they all showed tremendous compassion as I felt the need to talk, to talk endlessly about what had happened. Over a long lunch, they all sat with me in the staff restaurant, as we picked at the food and drank orange juice and coke, and listened as I poured out my heart. If they were uneasy, they never once showed it as I told the tale of Supi's death, the funeral, the press, the Diamond Cot Death Appeal, and the New Zealand trip.

Later, Chris took me aside. 'Of course, your friend Clare is right,' he said. 'You mustn't let Supi's death become bigger than his life. But look what you've been able to find out. Now what you can do is help make some *meaning* of his death.'

I got home that evening quite late. Oliver and Jamie were already in bed, and I was about to fall into mine, when the phone rang. It was my accountant, Russel Tenzer, the proud father of baby twins. 'I'm sorry to bother you – I know you've only just got back from New Zealand. I just wanted to know how you'd got on...'

So I told him. I was surprised I could condense it into thirty seconds – but there was really only one thing to tell the parent of young babies.

'So are you saying all babies should be put on their backs to sleep?' he double-checked with me.

'Yes.'

'And they could die if they're on their fronts?'

'In a word, yes.'

'My God! I won't keep you a moment longer.'

'Why – where are you going?'

'Upstairs, to turn the twins over.' And he put the phone down.

That's when I knew that our message could be *that simple, and that quick.*

Linda rang with the filming schedule for the next week. The documentary was scheduled for 30 October – just two weeks away. We still had the British side of the story to cover. First, we contacted the Department of Health to ask for a full statement on the truth behind what Ed Mitchell had told us – that the government had known all about their work. Then we asked for interviews with the ministers responsible. Then Austin Mitchell, Linda's MP husband, asked a question in the House of Commons about the New Zealand evidence. And finally, Linda released to the *Sun* a freeze-frame of me and the Maori baby, to keep up the media pressure.

Meanwhile, our next filming location was down the M5 in Bristol. Our New Zealand cameraman had flown over specially so that he could complete the documentary, rather than have a British cameraman take over. He had offered to continue the work free of charge because he was so committed to the subject – as long as we could pay his expenses.

Linda was driving. She had already arranged that we should interview a man called Dr Peter Fleming, a consultant paediatrician at St Michael's, the maternity hospital. At that time, as we were hurtling down the motorway at breakneck speed, I didn't think I could possibly meet anyone more inspirational than the New Zealand cot death experts. But here was a man whose quiet determination and stubborn courage had already saved hundreds of babies' lives.

Rather like the New Zealanders mysteriously finding themselves with the highest cot death rate in the world, Peter Fleming was practising medicine in an area – the county of Avon – which had the highest cot death rate in Britain. No-one knew why. But to a leading paediatrician, it was clearly a matter of great concern. So Peter found himself investigating the cot death problem with more vigour than many doctors elsewhere. Maybe it also had something to do with the fact that this caring man, slightly built with a shock of grey-white hair and a beard to match, was the father of four children. It must have worried him on a personal level that the area in which he was living with his doctor wife, Jo, had such a nightmare reputation for baby deaths.

He, too, set up a long-term study, investigating the children who had died and making direct comparisons with their 'controls' – similar children living nearby who had not died. This study had been funded mostly by the Foundation, though he was also supported by a smaller, locally-based charity, Cot Death Research.

The theory about sleep position had first been broached by an Australian paediatrician called Susan Beale, he explained, as we set up the camera and lights in his tiny, cramped office. 'She pestered me about it way back in May 1987, because she'd heard that I was about to start a big cot death study in Avon, and she wanted me to include a question about sleep position in my protocol of questions. Both she and Shirley Tonkin in New Zealand were becoming more and more convinced that sleep position had some sort of sinister importance – but, frankly, I was very doubtful. In the end, they nagged me so much that I agreed, so that I could investigate it and dismiss it.'

So no-one was more surprised than he when the evidence became startlingly clear. As in New Zealand, the babies who were dying were the ones on their tummies. And even those babies who had died, and had *not* been placed on their stomachs, had been *found* on their stomachs.

'It was overwhelming, I'm afraid,' Peter said. 'Maybe you can imagine my horror. Because the official advice to all mothers in this country was that babies should be put to sleep on their stomachs. It's in the government's official Baby Book, which is given to all new mums while they're in hospital. I had even been one of those doctors to recommend it to my own patients. I had even done it to my own sons. What I had discovered suddenly proved that we doctors had been wrong – and that advice was the cause of many needless deaths.'

Such an admission requires a great deal of honesty and courage, which is perhaps why Peter was booed off stage when he first delivered his message to cynical and even hostile medical audiences in lecture halls throughout the world. 'They thought I'd gone mad,' he said. 'But in actual fact, we in Avon had exposed a madness which was masquerading as medical fact. *There never was any proper medical reason for lying ordinary babies on their tummies. It was simply a fad – and unfortunately a dangerous one for some children. The idea that it saved some babies from choking on regurgitated milk is a myth put about probably by doctors seeking to justify their beliefs. There was never any medical basis for it.*'

So we mums had been sold a pup. My mind flashed back to a moment four years before, when my mother had stayed with me just after I had had Oliver. She had been shocked to see me put him down in his cot, on his tummy. 'I would never do that

176

with a baby,' she said. 'I was always told to put babies on their backs, or sides...'

'Oh, no!' I'd said, confidently. 'This is what you're meant to do – it's better for them.' If only I'd been the sort of girl who listened to her own mum, and hadn't read so many books.

If only we'd lived in Bristol. Because, by September 1989, Peter Fleming was so convinced of his data, and so depressed at the reaction of the rest of the medical fraternity, that he decided he would actively 'intervene' in the way Avon women brought up their babies. He would harness the local army of midwives, community nurses and health visitors, GPs and practice nurses, and he would start a local campaign telling mothers four vitally important points.

Number one was about sleep position. At first, he told mums to put their babies on their sides. He thought they would reject the message if it seemed too radical – and he knew many would be frightened to place their babies on their backs, the exact opposite of the official government advice. But within months, the incoming data on deaths convinced him he could go ahead with his 'back is best' message. Armed with a grant of several thousand pounds from the local cot death charity, he printed a hundred thousand leaflets. From autumn 1989 onwards, whenever a woman gave birth in the Avon district, she was told the new advice. Rarely did she ignore it, because it was backed up from every medical source, from her paediatrician to her family doctor.

Within six months, the cot death rate in Avon had almost halved. But still the rest of Britain ignored what was happening...' In fact, I was attacked,' said Peter. '*The Lancet* refused to publish my data and I was told by other scientists and doctors that my research work was unethical and unreliable because it dealt with people who had been newly bereaved. The reaction of the medical establishment was astonishingly blinkered.'

In the first quarter of the year, when they would normally

expect around sixteen or seventeen cot deaths, they got six. They knew then that they had quite literally hit upon a revolution in the history of cot death. That was in the first three months of 1990. It would be another nineteen months before mothers in the rest of the country would share such privileged information. God knows how many babies died in the United Kingdom in that period of time. Some three thousand? I was swaying on my feet. If the New Zealand story had been an emotional brickbat, then this dealt an even harder blow. While I was still only two months pregnant with Supi, Peter Fleming, just one hundred and twenty miles away from my front door, had upgraded his new advice to a full-blown local campaign, convincing mothers in Avon of an entirely different way of looking after their children. A simple piece of advice which was saving children. Though no-one knew which babies were being saved from cot death, it was obvious that some would have otherwise died.

Could Peter Fleming have saved the life of my little boy, had we lived in Avon? I cannot help but think yes, because it was particularly the 'classic' cases of cot death which were the first to almost disappear. As the picture built up over the ensuing months, and now years, there were fewer and fewer cases of four-month-old boys dying suddenly and unexpectedly, compared with the time before Peter's campaign. The cot deaths that were still happening tended to be the cases which were always the more unusual – children rather older than three or four months, children who were old enough to choose their own sleeping position.

What did Peter think of the New Zealand campaign? 'It absolutely reinforces everything I had found true of Avon,' said Peter. 'And while our area is relatively small, the New Zealand data covered a large area – and a whole country...'

That meant another thing to me – and to any doubters who might still exist after our documentary had gone out. If it worked in Avon, and it worked in New Zealand – how could it possibly fail to work in the whole of Britain? You didn't have to be a scientist or a doctor to know that, if we could mount a national campaign here in Britain, it *must* work. And that if we put all our efforts behind it, logically we should be able to follow the same pattern. We should be able to *halve* the cot death rate.

I took Peter to one side as the camera crew cleared up their things. 'What does this tell me about my baby?' I asked him quietly. 'Are you really telling me that my baby died simply because he was lying on his tummy – because I find that difficult to believe...'

Peter shook his head – and for the third, fourth or maybe even fifth time, a cot death expert took me by the arm and asked me if I really thought I should be doing all this, so soon after my baby's death. But I think Peter could see the desperation in my eyes. He recognized it from all the other newly bereaved mothers he'd met. We had to know why our babies had died. We just *had* to know. There would be no peace, no peace at all, until we knew.

'I cannot tell you exactly why your baby died,' he said sadly. 'We still do not know precisely what causes these babies to die. I only know that, for some babies, lying on their tummies is a huge risk factor. We know other risk factors – like overheating and parental smoking. But I cannot tell you much more than that – everything else is just theory. What we can do now, though, is give new babies a better chance than your baby had – a much better chance. We can reduce the risks. It works. But I cannot tell you how or why it works. *I just know that it does...*'

We said goodbye – and as we were turning to go, the phone rang from inside Peter's office. We left him as he returned to answer it. Minutes later, and while we were still loading our equipment on to a trolley, Peter came out to us, quietly smiling. 'I just thought you'd like to know...' he started, and then his voice sank to a conspiratorial whisper. 'That was the Chief

Medical Officer. He's asked me to join a special experts working party to urgently review the latest cot death data.'

My mouth dropped in amazement. So things were going to happen! 'Do you know who else he's asking?' I said.

'I know most of them already,' replied Peter. 'After all, there aren't many of us about. And you can be sure of one thing, it won't take us long to review research which we already know...' There was a look of confidence and sheer determination on his face.

Shortly after that meeting, I had a dream. It still haunts me, though less often now. In it, I am in a huge room, surrounded by hordes of men in white coats – so I presume they are doctors. Suddenly, the door opens and in rushes a man, also in a white coat, and he's waving a piece of paper. He's wildly excited, and he shouts: 'I've got it! I've got it!' And I know that he means he has found the answer to cot death – and it's on that piece of paper.

So I grab the paper from his hands, and run down the corridor with it. At the end of the corridor there's another room, an office, with a grey carpet, and a huge mahogany table. Sitting behind the dark table is an old man, with a very stern face. I flourish the piece of paper at him, and bring my fist down upon the table. 'Now,' I hiss at him. *'Now can I have my baby back?'* And that's where the dream ends every time. I've got to solve the mystery of cot death, so that I can have my baby back. That's what I kept thinking. There *will* be an end to this nightmare.

Chapter 20

'Let's make no bones about it,' said Linda. 'there will be one main reason people will watch this documentary – and it will be to see Anne Diamond cry.' She certainly had a way with words, did Linda. So when she set up the cameras and lights in our own living-room to shoot the final stage of our documentary, I was steeled against every trick she might play. I had done every other interview in the programme – but, of course, I couldn't interview Mike and myself. Now Linda turned the tables on me.

The crew, Jan and Linda hadn't actually heard the story of Supi's death. Not from our own mouths. Now we told them, as calmly as we could, while they recorded it. The house was hushed. We got to the end, and Linda patted us both on the back. She may not have got tears, but she knew she had some powerful material.

'If this documentary doesn't change things, I don't know what will,' she said. They turned off the lights, put the furniture back, and I went downstairs to the kitchen to make tea for everyone.

Linda turned the TV on. It was a big day in the television industry. The franchise awards were about to be announced. This was the ten-yearly fiasco where the ITV companies competed for the right to broadcast in their regions. For the first time, in true Thatcherite style, the franchises had been auctioned. They were to be awarded to the highest bidders. As I returned to the living-room with a trayful of tea and biscuits, the newsreader on *Sky News* started to deliver the bombshells. Thames TV had lost its franchise. So had TVS. So had TV-am.

Mike and I shot each other a look, and smiled ironically. That was the company for which I was making this documentary, the company for which I made *TV Weekly*, and my old employer! Oh dear! I wasn't doing too well!

Linda was whooping with delight. She was closely associated with one of the winners. My phone started ringing. All the people (and there were plenty of them) who had ever been fired by TV-am suddenly seemed to know my phone number. Henry Kelly, the TV presenter and game show host, rang. He had suffered under the ever-changing whims of Bruce Gyngell. 'So at last there is some justice in this world!' he crowed.

I thought of an old friend, Caroline Righton, who had also been fired after a contretemps with the Head of News, Bill Ludford. At the time, she had been very confused and upset. Though in a calmer moment she'd said: 'Ah, well... They do say that if you stand for long enough on the bridge, you will see the body of your enemy floating by...' I thought, with some satisfaction, how Caroline could now come down off her personal bridge.

Although the *Today* newspaper put me on the front page the next day, alongside former TV-am boss Greg Dyke, and called us 'The Avengers', I felt no satisafaction in watching TV-am lose its franchise, nor in seeing TV pictures of a shocked Bruce Gyngell and a disappointed David Frost. It had been a terrific company to work for, and I didn't regret a single minute I'd spent there. I was just sorry that I hadn't left on happier terms.

But all that seemed so unimportant now. It was, after all, only television. Supi's life and death had put things into proportion. The work I was doing now was possibly the greatest challenge of my career and my life. For Supi's sake, I had to get things changed.

In 1984, a Home Office pathologist made an unforgivable statement which he's lucky didn't get him lynched. He said that, in his opinion, most cot deaths were cases of parents smothering their own children. Remember his name – Dr Donald Wayte, just in case you ever meet him at a party. Throw a glass of red wine over him for me. His remark caused so much pain and nearly set cot death research back years. Coming from the lips of someone who was supposedly a caring and careful health professional, it also said a lot about the complacent attitude and harmful backwardness of establishment thinking.

The country's Chief Medical Officer at that time, Sir Donald Acheson, didn't exactly bend over backwards to remedy the harm, either. In fact, the situation was saved almost single-handedly by Princess Diana, who made a point by being seen very soon after at a function organized by the Foundation.

I just thank goodness that a more modern brain was in charge of the country's corporate health when we came back from New Zealand and Bristol. I strongly believe that if we hadn't had a new Chief Medical Officer – and the government had not been vulnerable in the run-up to a general election – nothing would ever have been done to change the official advice in the government's official *Pregnancy* and *Birth To Five* handbooks, babies in Britain would *still* be lying on their stomachs, and dying at the same appalling rate. Because there was almost a conspiracy of complacency in Britain about cot death. It was almost as though someone somewhere had decided that 2,000 deaths a year were somehow acceptable – a terrible tragedy, to be sure, but probably inevitable. After all, one prominent scientist had said to me, babies are very fragile. Throughout history, women had many babies, expecting only a few to survive. Maybe, he said, modern women had expectations which were too high.

Even the one big cot death charity in Britain, the Foundation for the Study of Infant Deaths, which had done such sterling work for the bereaved for the past two decades, had seriously failed when it had come to the crunch, because the Foundation had known about the sleeping position theory since the end of 1989. And from July 1990 they had convincing data, some would call it proof, from both New Zealand and Avon, that turning our babies on to their backs would save thousands of lives. By autumn 1990, they had had the new advice – telling us mothers to turn our babies over – printed up in draft leaflet form. It must have been sitting somewhere on a desk in Belgrave Square all through the spring and summer of 1991, while I had Sebastian.

We had been in constant contact with the Foundation. Indeed, they'd been one of the very first organizations which Linda and Jan had rung when we first planned the documentary. They were aware from the beginning that we were going to New Zealand, and why. While we were still there, and particularly after Ed Mitchell had spoken to us, we had rung the Foundation and asked for an interview upon our return. And while we prepared to go to their Belgrave Square offices to ask them some serious questions, they made an announcement which stopped us in our tracks. Linda went nuclear.

'I don't believe it, I simply don't believe it!' she ranted when she heard. 'The Foundation have suddenly decided they're going to hold a press conference to announce the risk reduction rules! I can hardly believe their nerve. They've had this information for the past two years, and suddenly while we're making a documentary about it, they decide to go public. And they're going to do it next week, would you believe? Just days before our programme goes out...'

There are, of course, two possible explanations for their behaviour. First, there's the one they asked us to believe. That it was a complete coincidence and they were going to announce the risk reduction rules at this time anyway. The second is that they had been embarrassed into action, and they didn't want to be shown up, in their very field of expertise, by some upstart of a bereaved mother and a nosey documentary crew.

All I know is I lost my baby while the Foundation withheld

184

information which could have saved his life. Countless other parents – it must run into thousands – lost their children while the Foundation – the very organization which *should* have served our interests on this subject – dithered over life-saving advice. When they were most needed, when they could have been most effective, the Foundation failed to act. We decided to meet them – and this time we called in our boss, the editor of Thames Television's *This Week*, under whose banner our documentary was to be broadcast.

I'd first met Paul Woolwich when I was a new reporter on the BBC evening programme, *Nationwide* – and he was a deputy editor. I hadn't really known him. Now, over this lunchtime meeting with Joyce Epstein and Dr Shireen Chantler, I was to see him show the mettle which had made him a serious force in the world of news and current affairs.

'He was brutal,' Linda said to me afterwards. I had thought he was brilliant. He had calmly but ruthlessly, over a three-course meal and coffee, put it to the two women that they had failed Britain's mothers once, and were about to do so again.

'You have been effectively withholding vital, life-saving information,' he told them, fixing them with a steely stare. 'Now you seek to disarm Anne as she prepares to pass on the medical advice which you ignored. Everything has been carefully planned to achieve maximum impact,' he explained to them. 'This isn't just any old documentary, this is co-ordinated with special editions of *Woman* magazine and the *Sun* so that we can reach as many mothers as possible, and create the biggest impact we can with the press. If you try to cover yourselves now, you will simply neutralize the impact, and water down the message.'

He didn't say it, but I could see in the faces of the two women a distinct recognition that they were being threatened with exposure. 'Is that what you really want?' hissed Paul. 'Or are you, perhaps, more interested in saving face than saving lives?'

And here I experienced what others in the political world

185

probably go through every day – the reaching of a compromise in order to safeguard the overall objective. We offered the Foundation the chance to sit alongside us when we previewed the documentary to the press. There, they could unveil their risk-reduction posters and leaflets, and we would seem to be united. In return, Linda and I agreed that we would not go too hard on them in the programme. Though I would have to ask them one question – the only one that really mattered...Why didn't they tell us about the life-saving discoveries that had been made in New Zealand?

Once again I sat in the Foundation's main office, opposite Joyce Epstein and Dr Shireen Chantler. But this time I was with a full TV crew. And this time, I knew an awful lot more about cot death than when I had last been there. The two women looked uncomfortable. They pointed out that they had discussed the risk-reduction formula, and specifically the sleep position data, in their newsletters. But, I retorted, people only receive their newsletter if they're on the mailing list. *In other words, you have to have had a cot death already.* Couldn't they see that that was hardly adequate? Why hadn't they told the rest of Britain?

The two women shuffled in their chairs and shot each other uncertain glances. 'Well, some of our doctors still don't agree about it...' started Dr Chantler.

So they wanted to wait for political unanimity within their organization before telling ordinary parents how to save the lives of their children?

'It's very difficult to know when to go public with new medical information,' said Joyce, emphatically.

And we left it there. In some respects, of course, she was right. It *is* difficult. But it wasn't too hard for the New Zealanders to know when they should tell the public. And, in the county of Avon, it wasn't too hard for Dr Peter Fleming to know when to change his advice for the mothers under his care.

The Foundation, however, still weren't convinced. I do not doubt the sincerity of their intentions. In many ways, the Foundation has provided much-needed solace and a focal point for the grief of thousands of bereaved parents. But by playing it safe in scientific terms, didn't they forget their human obligation? If they felt it safe to discuss the sleeping position theory in their newsletters, then why not in a campaign for all mothers? By the end of 1989, the doctor whose work they were funding, Peter Fleming, was totally convinced that changing sleeping position would save lives. By March 1990 he knew from experience that it also did no harm, that it was safe advice. If the Foundation wanted safety, they had it then. They could have safely hung on to the coat-tails of the New Zealanders, who had themselves starting campaigning in July 1990. But no. They hesitated and we parents lost.

But what about the people who were paid to do the job of looking after the nation's well-being – the Department of Health? We'd asked for an interview with the Secretary of State for Health, William Waldegrave, or with his Health Minister, Virginia Bottomley. *Why had they both said no?*

Chapter 21

'Being a Health Minister is like being a fireman,' Jeffrey Archer said to me, with a lavish gesture. His hand settled on the cushion of his vast sofa, in the centre of his enormous living-room, in his immense apartment overlooking the Thames. He beckoned me to sit down.

'You just have a series of fires to put out – and you turn your attention on the biggest and most dangerous first...What you've got to understand is that, after you, she's got a deputation from the AIDS charity, then the breast cancer people, then the leukaemia people, then the bone marrow people – and they all want the same thing, action and money. What you've got to do is get yourself first in the queue by making the most fuss. Then she'll do something simply to make you go away.'

I had gone to the millionaire author, desperately looking for political advice. I could not get any response from either William Waldegrave or Virginia Bottomley – and I wasn't just after an interview for the programme. That was essentially Linda's problem. What I wanted was an audience with one of them – so that I could convince them that we in Britain should start a cot death campaign – like the New Zealanders.

I had gone to Jeffrey because I knew he was friends with the Prime Minister, John Major. And, in my experience, if you couldn't get anywhere with the minions, you went straight to the top. I told Jeffrey about the New Zealand and Avon evidence. 'We could save over half the lives which are now lost, if only we set up a campaign,' I said. And, to appeal to him on another tack, I tried: 'And wouldn't it look good for your government to be the ones who'd done it? Just before a general election?'

Jeffrey leaned back and shouted over his shoulder to his secretary, who was sorting out books and paperwork on the massive glass table at the other end of the room. 'When am I having dinner with Virginia?'

'Next Thursday,' came the reply.

He turned back to me. 'Look. I'm meeting Virginia soon, so I'll collar her then. In the meantime, let me give you a few lessons on how to put pressure on a minister.'

I was all ears.

'First, you draw up a list of about ten friendly MPs – ones who will ask a question in the House for you...'

'Easy,' I said. I knew of at least a dozen who would help.

'Something along the lines of 'What is the minister doing about the cot death rate' would do. OK?'

'Yes.'

'Then you get someone rather more important, say a former minister – even better, a former Health Minister – someone like maybe David Owen – to table an early day motion along the same lines...'

'Yes, I think I can manage that...' I knew David Owen would at least be sympathetic. I had spoken to him about possibly chairing the Diamond Cot Death Appeal fund. He had been brimming with research ideas about cot death.

'And by then, the minister will be seriously worried about what is going on. Right? Then we go in for the...'

'Kill?' I ventured.

'Final stage...' he went on. 'And if Virginia won't see you then, I will try to get you the PM. But let's give this a go first...' Jeffrey kissed me on both cheeks and briskly walked me to the door. I knew he was a sincere friend, but I suspected that he, too, was something of a fireman. And I had been this morning's little blaze.

While the documentary rolled on towards the editing stage, Mike and I knew we could not wait to convince a government which might never budge. We knew we must do what the New

Zealanders had done – and if we had to do it by ourselves, then so be it. We must make a television ad – to tell British parents that their babies should be sleeping on their backs.

Shirley Tonkin had given me a video cassette copy of her own ad. She had pressed it firmly into my hands. 'If your government won't do it, then do it yourself,' she had said to me sternly. 'It's your profession, isn't it? It's what you're good at. If you can't do it, then who can?'

She was right. But how do you make an advert? Where do you start? Mike and I played the VHS over and over again – until we knew it word perfect. It starts with happy music, a softly lit sitting-room, and the TV presenter, Judy Bailey cradling a baby in her arms. 'New Zealand has the highest cot death rate in the world but there are things you can do to lower the risks for your baby.'

She bends, and puts the baby on his side in a large cot. 'Make sure you place your baby on his back or side to sleep – not his tummy. If he's on his side, have the underneath arm well forward so that if he rolls, he'll roll on to his back where he's quite safe.'

And then, smiling... 'It's very simple and it's one of the most important safety measures for your baby.' And that was it. Just thirty seconds, followed by a sponsorship logo of Phillips, the electronics giant.

'That's what we'll do,' said Mike, as he ran and re-ran the tape. 'We'll have to get sponsorship to pay for the airtime. Surely all the babywear and baby products manufacturers will help...' First though, we had to make the ad. Neither Mike nor I had ever made an advert before, and the discipline of shooting such stuff is quite different from the live, studio-type television we were used to. We both came from the world of news, where one reporter shoots an entire story with just one cameraman and a sound engineer. Adverts needed a cast from a different galaxy. People like 'dolly grips', 'gaffers', 'clapper loaders' and 'focus pullers'.

However, my agent, Jon Roseman, had once owned a company which made everything from pop videos to TV ads. We rang him, and within minutes he was assembling a team. I faxed the New Zealand script to his home, and his wife, Pearl, started work on a storyboard. Everyone concerned agreed to work either for free, expenses only, or for a reduced fee. But the hire of equipment, studios and editing suites would be costly. Mike and I thought that the advert could justifiably be made with money from the Diamond Cot Death Appeal, still running in the *Sun*. We rang Kelvin MacKenzie, the editor, and told him the plan. 'Great!' he said. 'We'll support you all the way.' And he promised he would arrange for the money to be extracted from the charitable trust. Apparently, though the Charity Commissioners had been informed, the change of directors and change of use from the old charity name had still not been formalized.

'What?' yelled Mike at Kelvin. 'How come that has taken so long?'

Kelvin sighed down the phone. 'Come on, Mike, you know what lawyers are like...'

We were advised that it would take months if we waited for the paperwork to catch up with us – so the *Sun*'s lawyers set to work contacting the old directors, to get their permission for the money to be used. It was days before we heard anything. We kept ringing Kelvin. He returned our calls, only to sound more exasperated every time. 'Look. I feel as frustrated as you two...' Backwards and forwards went faxes, confirming the filming arrangements for the ad, its costs, its content, its aims and purposes. Still no cheque.

We wrote the script, copying exactly the New Zealand words, but with changes pertinent to Britain. Peter Fleming, in Bristol, approved the final draft. 'By the way,' he said, as we went through the script for the last time, 'I've heard again from the Department of Health. The expert working party meets next week, just about when your documentary goes out.'

Clearly this new Chief Medical Officer was not going to waste time. Maybe, he, too, was a fireman, angry that he had inherited such an explosive situation.

Now we had to get our ad passed by the ITC, the watchdog committee set up to safeguard standards. They quibbled over our figures. Was it 'nearly five' children dying every day of cot death in Britain, or 'over four'? Figures differed between the Foundation's numbers and the government's. Finally, we settled for 'at least four'.

We faxed the ITC approval to the *Sun*'s lawyers. Still no cheque.

I was adamant that our advert should feel optimistic rather than scarey, so we needed something upbeat to counterbalance the sad statistics. I knew just what I wanted. I tried it out on Mike...

'Do you think we could play a snatch of Elton John at the end of the ad? The bit from "Your Song", where he sings, "how wonderful life is while you're in the world..." Don't you think it would be nice?'

'Let's give John Reid a ring,' said Mike. John Reid was Elton's manager, and a friend of ours. Within a couple of hours, we had the message that Elton would be delighted to let us play the extract, free of charge, as long as the record company agreed. Very soon we had the confirmation we needed. It was all go. We faxed everything to the *Sun*'s lawyers.

Still no cheque. We were in danger of having to cancel the shoot, so in desperation, I rang the lawyers myself. The man I wanted was, of course, unavailable, so I screeched at his poor partner. 'Have you got children? Don't you realize that if we have to delay this advert you and your partner will have babies' lives on your conscience? Because every day we delay now, babies will be needlessly dying...'

It got me nowhere. We rang Kelvin. 'Don't start at me,' he sighed. 'I'm only the editor. You may think that's powerful, but it's nothing compared to lawyers...'

Just two days later, we found out what may have so preoccupied those lawyers. They were also the Queen's lawyers. And the very next day, the Duke and Duchess of York announced their separation. We went ahead and made the ad – and the money was released just in time.

It was beautifully lit – you couldn't see a trace of my anxiety or tiredness. And the baby – from a modelling agency – looked absolutely gorgeous. 'Every day in Britain,' I said to the camera, 'at least four babies die from cot death. New research shows you can reduce the risks for your baby. Sleep him on his back or side, not on his tummy. If he's on his side, have the underneath arm well forward so that if he rolls – he'll be on his back, where he's safe. This is not a cure but it really can help save your family from the tragedy of losing a precious young life...' And then Elton John took up the theme: 'How wonderful life is while you're in the world.'

But who were we to give out new medical advice? Since when did Anne Diamond and Mike Hollingsworth get their medical degrees? We knew we couldn't broadcast the ad without an endorsement from a reputable medical body. We couldn't even get to see the Health Minister. So it had to be the Foundation.

We rang Joyce Epstein. Would the Foundation accept the ad as a gift? In return, would they endorse it? We told them our plan. We would somehow (we didn't yet know how) find a sponsor. And then we would air the ad at a time when it would be seen by the most people, and create the most publicity – the *Coronation Street* advertisement break. In TV, if you want to achieve maximum sales, then you advertise around *Coronation Street* or *News at Ten*.

We knew that the airtime was expensive. But if things worked according to plan, we shouldn't have to pay for the ad after that. Because we would use the publicity to embarrass the government into adopting the ad themselves. There was just the sticky problem of finding a sponsor with enough money...

The girl from Mothercare gulped when I told her. 'How much?' she asked again, incredulous.

'£58,000,' I said, meekly.

'That's more than we've got left in the whole advertising budget,' she answered. 'There's no way...'

I interrupted quickly. 'We're going to try and get the TV companies to reduce their fees,' I told her.

'Yes, surely, for a charity they'll come right down...'

We knew we'd got Mothercare interested. But they hadn't been expecting to cough up quite so much dough. Not for just thirty seconds.

Luckily, an advertising expert from the *Sun*'s ad agency had offered to help. He was called Paul Booth, and he guided Mike and myself through what was to us virgin territory. Firstly – how were the TV tariffs set? It seemed by market forces only. In other words, the TV companies all charged individually to advertise in their own regions, and it seemed they could charge whatever they liked. Peak airtime was very popular, and the highest bidder won the time. So how could we get them to reduce their fees just for us? 'We're just going to have to ring round every company and beg,' said Paul. And the three of us sat down at the phones.

If Supi's death had made front-page headlines at the time, then cot death was even bigger news now, in the warm-up to the release of our documentary. So the advertising managers in most of the ITV areas knew immediately why our ad was so important, and were sympathetic. We were doing well. Every company had agreed a sizeable reduction – some had halved their normal rate. Every company, that is, except Thames and Central. 'I know the managing directors of both those companies!' I said eagerly. 'Let me see if I can try a bit of personal charm!'

I rang straight through to the managing director of Thames TV, Richard Dunn. He knew why I was ringing. I pointed out to him that our documentary was being broadcast under his company name. That he *had* to be able to do something.

He wasted no time on words.

'Leave it to me, Anne. I can't promise anything. Advertising people are a law unto themselves. But I'll try.'

Within the hour, we had a message that Thames would reduce their rate. But we had no such luck with Central.

Despite my appealing directly to the director of news and current affairs, Bob Southgate (who promised to take it higher), Central refused to budge. This was the company which had just bought its entire franchise for £2,000, while others had had to pay millions. This was the company for which I had once worked. If Lew Grade had still been in charge, they would have responded, I thought. But now it seemed that it was just run by money men, with no soul.

Mothercare, through their public relations lady, Jane Cookham, had indicated that they would pay, if we could get the cost down to £25,000. We were in trouble. We had booked the spot for Monday, 4 November on Thames, Granada, Yorkshire, Tyne-Tees, STV, Grampian, TVS/Channel, HTV and Anglia at a total cost of £27,327.50. There were no other sponsors around. For Mothercare, we were already over budget. And we simply couldn't afford the extra £17,000 wanted by Central.

Jane at Mothercare was unhappy. So was I. 'I don't think it would be right for us to broadcast a life-saving message to everyone except mothers in the Midlands,' she said. 'I don't know what more we can do...'

'I do,' said Mike. 'We'll run the ad everywhere else in Britain, and then you and I can go on *Central Weekend*, the Friday night show. They've been asking us if we'll do it. Let's tell them we will, so long as they show our ad in their programme.'

It seemed like the perfect solution.

Chapter 22

I knew the documentary was going to be successful when I saw tears in the eyes of a Fleet Street girl reporter. It was preview day, and every newspaper had sent someone to see it. This particular girl reporter – long, leggy, blonde and about thirty years old – came up to me afterwards. 'I've got to rush to file my copy,' she said, and then, in an embarrassed gush: *'I just want you to know that if I ever have a baby of my own, I will make sure that it sleeps on its back!'*

With that, the tears came – to both of us – and she clenched my hand quickly, and then left. And that reaction was exactly why we had made the documentary – to tell everyone that at last there was something you could do about cot death. Not just mothers – but *future* mothers. And fathers.

We had called it 'Every Mother's Nightmare' because that was what Nanny Sandra had said when she first arrived on that fateful day – and it's how everyone sought to describe it. I received lots of complaints, though, from fathers who pointed out that cot death was every *father's* nightmare, too. And, of course, it is. It's just that 'Every Parent's Nightmare' didn't have the same ring to it.

The next day was transmission day. It was also Hallowe'en, and the children had invited friends around for a spook party (liquorice spiders and green cake and the like). It was also *TV Weekly* day – and I had a hectic schedule. I left home at 6.30am to drive to Southampton. I'd be at the TVS studios by 9am, and straight into a production meeting. After a couple of coffees, I'd go into the studio, where we would rehearse as much as possible – and then into make-up. Then came the highlight of the day – a long working lunch, when we'd meet the guest, and go over the interview. Today it was Desmond Morris and Sarah Kennedy. Then we'd go back to the studio for a live transmission. *TV Weekly* was a lovely, fun programme – and the production team very close. They were bubbling with excitement, of course, about the news that TVS was to lose its franchise. What would they do? Become an independent company? Would the new franchise holder want to commission any more *TV Weekly*s?

After the programme was transmitted, we all met back in the Green Room for a glass of wine before going our separate ways. Everyone was talking about their future. I was preparing to dash, in order to make it home in time for the Hallowe'en tea, when the phone rang. Chris Riley, the editor, answered it, and spoke briefly. He looked over to me, and cupped his hand over the mouthpiece.

'It's for you. Someone from the Press Association. Says they want to speak to you – about cot death.'

I took the phone. A female voice greeted me. 'Hello, Anne, I just wanted your reaction to the news...'

'What news?' I asked, nervously. I sensed the room go silent around me.

'Well, we've just had a statement from the Department of Health. Basically, it says that the expert working party has met and decided that *from now on, all babies in Britain should be laid to sleep on their backs...*'

Chris saw my face – and he walked over and sat in the chair next to me. 'Are you all right?'

'Yes,' I said quietly, and looked up at him. 'The Department of Health has just said that all babies should sleep on their backs. From today onwards!'

The room erupted. Everyone, TV producers, directors, researchers – people who'd never changed a nappy in their lives – they all knew how important it was.

'Hello? Hello?' said the voice at the other end of the phone.

'Are you there? Can I ask you how you feel about this?'

I turned my attention back to the lady from the Press Association 'It's wonderful news, simply wonderful!' I said, and burst into tears.

The mobile phone was pretty busy in my car that evening, as I made my way home. Linda was ecstatic – and was hastily editing the Department of Health's statement onto the end of our programme. I rang Peter Fleming in Bristol. 'It was easy,' he said. 'The Chief Medical Officer gave us about six weeks to review all the latest research but it took us just one afternoon... It's wonderful, Anne. And it wouldn't have happened without this sort of pressure.'

But we both knew that the fight couldn't end there. It wasn't enough for the Chief Medical Officer to change the rules. What we needed now was a massive campaign to tell parents all about it.

The Hallowe'en party was almost a late birthday party for Oliver. It had not been intended as such, but the guest list inevitably included many little friends who had been invited in July, and who had been cancelled. They realized this, and brought presents – so Oliver had an unexpected boost to the proceedings. Smartie Arty came to entertain – though his eyes rolled skywards when he saw a room full of witches, wizards, ghosts and creepy crawlies. 'Aaaah!' he moaned. 'They're always more difficult to control when they're dressed up!' When the last cup of blood and the final worm sandwich had been consumed, and the children yawned their way off home, Mike and I slipped on our jackets to go down to Thames Television.

The documentary was to go out at 8.30. Before transmission, there was to be a small reception for everyone concerned. We both felt that we should be there, to thank the cast and crew. But we both wanted to be at home when the programme went to air. For the team, no matter how committed they had been, it was another programme. For us, it was Supi's life –

and our attempt to make some meaning of his death. We knew we would find it too emotional to witness in front of colleagues.

Paul Woolwich, *This Week*'s editor, offered me a glass of wine. His family, too, had suffered a near-miss cot death – and he had witnessed the family anguish it had caused. 'I just want to say well done. I know how hard it must have been. And just look at what has happened today. Things have already changed...'

Paul and I had had long discussions, over a couple of lunches, about life and the cosmos. Since our *Nationwide* days, we had gone very separate ways. He had pursued more serious current affairs television. I, meanwhile, had gone into 'tabloid television', and become what the papers called a 'star'. He knew my concerns about that. 'But if you ever wondered why you became "famous", now you know...' he added. 'This was it, wasn't it? You couldn't have achieved any of this if you hadn't been famous.'

We went home quietly, and watched the programme downstairs in the playroom with Mike's parents sitting, sobbing, on the red sofa. As the end titles started rolling, a voice-over announced that, from this day onwards, the advice given to every new parent was to be changed. British babies should now sleep on their backs or sides.

The phone rang – the first of many times that evening.

It was my mum. 'That was good,' she said simply. And it was. I played a part in it, but it was a monumental team effort – and the leader of that team was Linda. It had been her idea in the first place, and her sheer energy had built it into a powerful piece of television. Linda saved a great many lives that night, and I never thought to tell her so. I was hardly objective at the time – but later I came to realize that I was more proud of making that programme than practically anything else I have ever done in my career.

That documentary should have won an award.

Unfortunately, because of stupid TV politics, it was never entered for one. We could not, however, stop to think about that. We were in campaigning mode.

We had been invited on to the debate programme, *The Time The Place*, the following morning – but I was adamant we should refuse to take part. Its style was altogether too confrontational. It prided itself on being a British version of the *Phil Donaghue Show* or the *Oprah Winfrey Show*, but it was a poor copy. It merely opened up subjects for debate – and invited people to contradict each other. I knew I couldn't face that.

However, the ITV network mid-morning magazine, *This Morning*, had also invited us to appear. They occupied the next slot in the ITV morning schedule. We agreed, providing that they promised to show our ad, which was now edited and ready. So armed with a copy, we flew to Liverpool to be interviewed by husband and wife team Richard Madeley and Judy Finnigan. We knew that *This Morning*'s audience was largely mothers with small children. The sort who would be interested in our message. And the sort who would pass it onto others.

Richard and Judy were kind, and concerned. It shocked me that they hadn't seen our documentary the night before. But I quickly checked myself. When I had been on TV-am, no way could I always watch the programme or read the book which my guest had come on to 'plug'. It simply isn't possible – not when you're interviewing four or five people every day. Not when you have a family of your own at home, kids to bath and homework to help with, as Richard and Judy had. I realized that though Supi's death and our cot death crusade was *everything* to us, it was just another story to the rest of the media. We would have to work hard, and quickly, before the media got fed up with us, as they inevitably would.

So – cot death had been debated on *The Time The Place*, on *This Morning* and now we were off to Central TV to appear on their evening programme, *Central Weekend*. This was also a

201

highly confrontational debate programme, and my instincts warned me against it. But we had agreed to appear for two reasons. First, because they had agreed to show our advert. And it was the only way we would be able to ensure that mothers in the Central area would have the chance to view it. Second, because the programme's producers had agreed to fly Shirley Tonkin over from New Zealand. I knew she would be a powerful ally in our fight to get a full-scale cot death campaign out of the government. But it was a horrid programme. Its logo was the silhouette of two people yelling at each other.

We travelled by car from *This Morning*'s Liverpool studios to Birmingham, where the Central studios were squashed in between several large Brummie roundabouts, a couple of flyovers and a six-lane highway. En route, both Mike and I were busy on our separate mobile phones. Mothercare were still fainting at the price of showing the ad. We had tried everything we could think of to reduce the price still further, but to no avail. Now we were trying other ideas for sponsors. Paul Booth, our advertising friend at Arc, was going through his book of likely sponsors. We thought that, since the publicity was now at an all time high, we might be lucky.

We were just nearing the outskirts of Birmingham when Jane Cookham phoned from Mothercare. 'Sorry I've been so long getting back to you, but it's because they've held a special board meeting because they were worried about broadcasting the ad to mothers everywhere except the Central region.'

We understood their problem – but hadn't we got around that, by having the ad played out on *Central Weekend*?

'Well, I'm afraid the board thought that that wasn't good enough. Either it would have to be broadcast to everyone, or morally, Mothercare shouldn't sponsor it.'

My heart sank. Were they going to pull out?

'So the board has just met. And they've agreed to pay for the full country, including Central. Though will you try and get the price down a bit further if you can?'

We whooped with delight. We rang Paul Booth at Arc straight away, and told him to confirm everything for the play-out at three minutes to eight, just after the Monday edition of *Coronation Street*.

We arrived at the Central studios, but only just in time. A producer met us at reception, and whisked us along the corridor towards make-up. 'There's just one problem,' he said as he flung us in the doors, where two make-up artists were waiting. 'I'm afraid we cannot show your ad for various technical reasons. So we've got a live baby for you instead.'

It was the dirtiest of TV tricks. Technical problems, my foot. They had just decided a live demonstration would be more fun. And it might even make Anne Diamond cry. They had blatantly contravened our basic agreement – to show the ad. What felt even worse was that the baby to be used as a prop was the tiny daughter of the show's presenter, Anna Soubry. There was no time to argue about it, because within minutes we were on air.

'Are you OK?' asked Mike, worried that I might be unnerved by having to handle a baby in public so soon after Supi's death. I was angry – but I could cope. And I was damned if they were going to make me cry.

They had set up a cot in one area of the studio, and asked me to demonstrate the new advice. I walked over to the cot, furiously thinking how I could turn this situation, cunningly designed to turn me into a victim, to my satisfaction. Anna Soubry handed me her little baby daughter. She was about four months old. I was careful not to flinch, though I could feel all eyes on me. Then I turned to Shirley Tonkin, who was sitting in the audience, and I invited her to come on to the studio floor with me.

'Now, Shirley, you explain what the new advice is...' And Shirley, ever the professional, talked me through it. At the end, I announced that our ad would be transmitted the following Monday, sponsored by Mothercare.

There was loud applause. I returned to my seat on the studio plinth, and Shirley returned to hers in the audience. Mike gripped my hand tightly. 'Well done,' he said. And the debate went on. I didn't hear another word. I was shaking with anger. But at least I had got the message across.

On the way out of the studio, I crossed paths with a woman I instantly recognized as Edwina Currie, the outspoken MP and former Junior Health Minister. Edwina was as famous for 'putting her foot in it' as for her political career. In fact, one had led nearly to the end of the other. She had lost her job in the ministry when she'd declared that most of Britain's eggs contained salmonella. It was a fact which most people perceived to be absolutely true, but she had to resign anyway.

Now Edwina put her foot in it again. She was waiting in the wings to go on air and debate the next subject in the show. But she saw me, walked over and patted me sweetly on the tummy. 'Congratulations, Anne! I didn't know you were expecting another!' I was dumbstruck, smiled stupidly and walked on. I heard a floor manager take her aside and point out to her that I'd only just had a baby, three months ago, and that had been the one which had died.

Maybe that's why, after the programme ended, Edwina made a beeline for me in the Green Room. It wasn't like her to apologize – but instead she offered to do something much more useful. 'I can get you in to see the Health Minister,' she said. 'I'll fix it up, and give you a call.'

Meanwhile, Mike was enjoying a large glass of wine with Shirley Tonkin. She had spent the day with Dr Kenneth Calman, the Chief Medical Officer. 'He wants to see you,' she said. 'They're still not convinced they need to do a campaign. They think they can just tell mothers through doctor's surgeries and maternity wards... You've got to convince them, Anne. This sort of message needs television. Just like we did it, only bigger and better.'

She gave me that look again. That platinum steel glare

which must have withered a thousand medical students and beat hundreds of problem children into meek submission.

'If you don't do it, who else is going to?'

Chapter 23

There are hidden costs in making a TV ad. No-one tells you that it takes time and money simply editing a Mothercare logo on to the end. No-one tells you that you have to book studio time simply to play the cassette on a machine, and send it up the telecommunications lines to every major ITV station. And no-one tells you that you have to pay for the cassette tape which records it at the other end. We were physically exhausted and at the end of our mental tethers by the time we'd had it confirmed that every ITV station was ready to play it out.

We watched every frame of *Coronation Street* that night. After the middle commercial break, our phone rang. Half of our family and friends had got it wrong, and had been watching the wrong commercial break. 'Where was it?' they cried.

So we all waited with bated breath for 7.57pm. Suddenly, there it was – between a baked beans commercial and another one for washing powder. And suddenly there it was – gone. The most expensive thirty seconds I'd ever been responsible for. Nearly £45,000 (including VAT) gone – just like that. I hoped someone had noticed it. Because we all felt a huge anti-climax. The only time I'd ever spent so much, so quickly, was when I had bought a house. But at least then I had had something to show for it. Now, we just felt empty. 'God,' exclaimed Mike. 'I hope that has the effect we planned.'

We went to bed that night, comforting each other that all advertisers must feel that way. But it must work, or the washing powder people wouldn't do it so much. And if that ad break was to result in increased sales of Ariel, then it should also cause increased awareness of our life-saving campaign.

The next morning, the newspapers responded – particularly interested in the angle that Elton John had given us a few bars of 'Your Song'. And by breakfast time we were inundated with requests for interviews. We went on TV and radio, to put the same point, over and over again. *Why should we British parents accept such shoddy treatment from our Department of Health? If New Zealand babies were worth saving, then why were British babies being so short-changed? We need a campaign and we need one now.* It was deliberately emotive stuff – real 'soundbite' material, but we could sense it was working.

We appeared on the BBC mid morning TV show *UK Today*, hosted by Miriam Stoppard, a TV doctor. She shook us heartily by the hand. 'You know we doctors have known about this sleeping position thing for years. It's absolutely disgusting that we've never done anything about it. I think the medical profession has a lot to be ashamed about. It shouldn't have had to take a celebrity's child to die...'

While we were driving back from the TV studio, near Westminster, the car-phone rang. It was the Chief Medical Officer, Dr Kenneth Calman's secretary. Could we make a meeting with him soon? A few days later, we arrived at his office in Whitehall. Mike had a VHS copy of our ad carefully tucked under his arm. Dr Calman, a genial Scot who was quick to tell us that he, too, was a father, met us with a warm handshake.

'I've been following what you've done, and I admire your courage,' he said.

That was a good start, I thought. At least the man is not hostile.

'Now tell me what you think we should be doing.'

Over a civilized cup of coffee and biscuits, we explained what had inspired us most about the approach being taken in New Zealand, and about Peter Fleming's local campaign in Avon.

'You medical men have done your work now,' Mike said. 'You've concluded that back is best. Now you must leave it to the communicators to get the message across...'

We explained, in as simple language as we could without sounding patronizing, that we were pretty experienced in broadcasting to the very audience that he needed to reach. We'd spent our whole careers in that very field. We showed him our tape.

'Can I keep this copy?' he asked.

We were only too delighted. Were we getting somewhere? Or was he another fireman intent on extinguishing a spark before it blew up into a damned great fire? In other words, was that the last we'd ever hear from him? I put it to Mike as we left Richmond House, the Department of Health building in Whitehall, and hailed a taxi to go home.

'No, I don't think so,' said Mike. 'He must recognize that this is no longer a little fire. It's already a bloody great inferno. And if I were him, just weeks into a new job, I wouldn't want to start my period of office in a burned-out wreck...'

The next day, Edwina Currie called. 'Can you make next Tuesday, 5.30pm?' she asked. She had got us in to see Virginia Bottomley.

Mike and I arrived at Richmond House reception with another VHS tape under our arms, and our brains well-tuned for an argument. Peter Fleming arrived with his assistant, Alison Stewart, and a brief-case full of research documents. They had spanking new research material (just completed), which showed that they had reduced the cot death rate in Avon by an overall seventy-five per cent since they had first started the new advice. We all had an expectant glow. Edwina came rushing up to meet us, looking brisk and puffed-up, like a headmistress in charge of a speech day. She almost dusted us off and straightened our ties, as we waited to be shown into the Inner Sanctum. It was a waiting-room, off a waiting-room, off another waiting-room. This was more nerve-wracking than going to see the Queen.

Eventually, we passed through an enormous oak door, and there, at the other end of a gigantic polished table, sat Virginia Bottomley with her famous smile. She was flanked one one side by her Chief Press Officer, Philip Aylett, and on the other by Romela Christopherson, her public relations officer. Edwina started to grovel. I hadn't expected such obsequiousness from the Member for Derbyshire South.

'Minister,' she grovelled. 'Thank you so much for sparing us a few minutes in your hectic schedule. Can I introduce...' Well, I hadn't exactly expected 'Hi, Ginny!' But this took me quite aback.

It was then I realized that we were indeed now meeting the Fire Chief. This was an exercise designed to smother our militant flames in a blanket of drool. We were clearly meant to shake the all-powerful hand, and then go home with a nice, rosy feeling that we had done our best. That we had gone to the top. Mike, Peter and I shot each other knowing looks. It was now or never. We brushed aside the small talk. If we were only being allotted a few minutes in the Health Minister's busy timetable, then we would waste no time.

'All the research from New Zealand and Avon shows that the cot death rate drops at least by fifty per cent in the first six months following a campaign,' I started. 'And it gets better. The figures then go on to show that the rate can drop still further in the next six-month period.'

Mrs Bottomley looked impressed for a second. 'How do those statistics translate into British figures?' she asked.

It's now or never, I thought. And I could hear Shirley Tonkin nagging in my ear... 'We are losing two thousand babies a year in the UK,' I said firmly. 'That's about four a day. So, with a properly targeted campaign, we could...' and then I corrected myself... '*you*...could save...three of them.'

I knew it sounded too simple. She leaned back in her chair,

and that smile returned. She turned away from me. Maybe she suspected I was talking journalistic hype. She looked at Peter.

'Surely not?'

Peter nodded. 'It's absolutely right. That's what the evidence says. It's been done in New Zealand, and I have done it myself in Avon.'

She raised her eyebrows for a moment's thought. 'I see...suppose we did do a campaign. How and where would we do it?'

Peter told her how he had mounted his campaign in Avon. And then Mike and I launched into our case for television. Peter agreed. It was the only way to successfully reach the whole nation. We were asking a whole generation of people to unlearn what had previously been taught. We were also asking a generation of doctors, midwives and health visitors to accept that what they had taught in the past was wrong. There would be pockets of opposition, of complacency and doubt. The only way to counter that was by creating a demand for the information from the mothers themselves.

'And the only way to get that sort of saturation marketing is television,' said Mike.

Mrs Bottomley turned white. 'Oh, no!' she butted in, with a dismissive hand. 'We couldn't possibly afford to use television...'

At this, Edwina chipped in. 'Oh, that's a pity, minister... Not even in the spring or summer, when the advertising rates are cheap?'

We were prepared for this one. Mike got the VHS tape out, and we outlined a plan for using the ad we had already made, and harnessing commercial sponsors. We had even had one famous children's cartoon character offered to us to help promote posters and leaflets.

'It's not just a financial consideration,' replied the minister. 'I don't believe that TV is necessary. Newspapers and baby magazines are the way to reach young mothers. Young mums don't watch television.'

This was unbelievable. I turned around to see if Mike was still beside me, half expecting to see that he'd fainted to the floor in sheer disbelief.

'No?' I said to the Minister... 'Then who watches *Neighbours*, *Home and Away*, *This Morning* and *TV-am*? Who watches *EastEnders* and *Coronation Street*, *The Price Is Right* and *Blind Date*?'

She looked blank. Maybe she thought I had lapsed into a foreign language. I was just about to launch into my theory about washing powder advertisers, when I was stopped. Edwina was up, and dusting us off again. I was actually still saying something when she pulled the chair out from underneath my bottom, and prepared to whisk me off.

'Right, well, we're so very grateful, minister, for your time. I know you're very busy so we won't keep you a moment longer. But thank you so much...' she said.

I was horrified. I could say that it was like being back at primary school, except that I don't ever remember being herded in such a way even then. I turned my back on Edwina, and faced Mrs Bottomley head on. 'So what is going to happen now?' I asked point blank.

She rose to her full height, and her lieutenants closed in. 'I think we all agree that we need to disseminate this new information to the public in as effective a form as possible. And I agree, that should probably be in the form of some sort of campaign in the printed media.'

'And what about TV coverage?' I asked. 'We all seem to agree that TV and radio is vital to its success, don't we?'

'Well, no, frankly I am not convinced... And anyway,' she added, smiling benevolently. *'You already seem to be achieving that very well for us...'*

I saw red, and brought my fist down on the table. 'No!' I said. 'No! That simply is not good enough!'

Mike brought his hand down next to mine. 'No!' he echoed. 'We will not go on exposing our private grief in public just in order to save you money. If you want our professional help, then we will gladly give it. But we will not continue to prostitute our grief.'

Edwina shuffled awkwardly, and made noises again to leave. Mrs Bottomley smiled again. 'We'll mull over everything you said,' she promised. 'And we will get back to you. I promise...we will get back to you...'

Chapter 24

She kept her word. Two days later, her letter arrived in the morning post. In it, she explained that the Department of Health would produce a printed leaflet: 'This message must be communicated professionally and in some detail. We will be using national newspaper advertising and ensuring that the concerned medical, nursing and voluntary organizations collaborate in the initiative...'

'In other words,' explained Peter Fleming, when I rang him, 'they're going to do no more than the absolute minimum.'

I just could not understand it. We couldn't have made it any plainer. We had outlined a simple formula which was almost guaranteed to save hundreds of lives, and yet they didn't really want to know. Couldn't they see, even at the basest level, the incredible public relations value of such a campaign? Especially before a general election? Their attitude seemed so cheapskate. I was depressed. I had put my all into that deputation to the minister. Maybe, I thought now, maybe I was wrong to have lost my temper.

But Mike was angry. He stormed to the phone, and got through to Philip Aylett, the man who had been at Mrs Bottomley's left hand. They started talking. I could tell that Mike was becoming agitated. At one point, he threatened to come to blows. Finally, he slammed the phone down.

'I don't believe it!' he spouted. 'That man is trying to rewrite history. He's airbrushed out everything we achieved at that last meeting. He denies nearly everything that happened. He says there was never any talk of using TV in the campaign... Honestly, it's just like that sit-com *Yes, Minister*. These civil servants think they can turn black into white. They think they can manipulate everyone. Well, he's not getting away with it.'

We both sat down at the word processor, and constructed a furious letter to Mrs Bottomley. By now we'd been invited on to more TV and radio shows. We had declined them for fear of offending Mrs Bottomley, as she planned her cot death initiative. Now we felt we had something more to say.

In the newspapers, on radio and again on TV, in Miriam Stoppard's show, we were asked the same question: 'Isn't it great that the Department of Health has finally announced a cot death information campaign?'

'No, it is not great,' we replied. 'The government is doing only the moral minimum. In New Zealand they had a TV campaign. British babies deserve the same.'

Three cheers for the British media. Mrs Bottomley's office was on the phone the next morning. Could we come down to Whitehall straight away? As we caught another cab – it was impossible to park anywhere near Whitehall so we couldn't drive our own car – I wondered if Mrs Bottomley had even thought of how we could afford to drop everything and come at her command. It cost a fortune in cab fares.

When we got to her office, she was sitting again at the big table. This time, she had an array of press cuttings in front of her, and she was tapping them, in an irritated manner, with her fingernail. 'This will not do,' she said. 'This will not do...'

I could see they were cuttings about our most recent TV and radio utterances.

'This sort of discord will not do. We must be seen to show a united front.'

We sat down. What was she going to say? Was she simply going to tell us off?

She continued tapping, obviously annoyed. 'I told you the last time we met that I do not consider TV coverage necessary to this campaign. Frankly, I have to say, that is still my opinion...'

I sat on the edge of my chair.

'But I have been persuaded, against my better judgement, that we *should* make a television advert. And we would very much like it if you would agree to present it for us.'

I looked her hard in the eyes. They were icy blue. It was impossible to tell if she was happy or angry. But across the table, Romela Christopherson beamed. I looked at Mike. I could tell that he was trying as hard as me to stop a cry of delight. Dammit, I thought, I'm not going to give her that satisfaction.

'Why not use the ad we've already made?' I asked.

'Well, we've looked at it, and taken all the due advice. And we believe it doesn't go far enough. We think we can now go one better than the New Zealanders. We can tell British mothers that back is best.'

It was true. All the research from New Zealand and Avon now showed that the advice should be to lay babies down on their backs. The half-way advice of lying on the side was now outdated. We in Britain could confidently go the whole hog.

Mrs Bottomley turned to Romela. 'Shall we show them the logo?'

Romela uncovered a large piece of artwork which had been lying on the table in front of her. It was a huge white square, with a grey cartoon of a baby asleep, on its back. The baby made the shape of a capital 'B', and it was lying on a bed of three letters, A, C and K.

'The campaign will be called 'Back to Sleep'. I rather like it. What do you think?' Mrs Bottomley asked.

Mike looked distinctly unimpressed. He said later that he couldn't understand why anyone would call a campaign 'Ack to Sleep', and I couldn't help but agree. The graphics were a bit confusing. Still, it had been rushed out.

'Now, will you agree to front the TV ad for us?' asked Mrs B. again.

I wanted to jump up and shout *Yes, of course I will! Isn't that what I've been on about for days?* Instead I heard myself saying: 'Can I think about it?'

'What did you say that for?' asked Mike as we walked back to reception.

'I don't really know,' I answered. 'But I'm damned if I'm going to lick her hand.'

When the government wants to spend money, it can spend money. They didn't hire just any old TV crew to make this ad. They hired the best. The director was the internationally famous photographer, Terence Donovan. It was a huge studio, positively awash with production talent. And they'd hired six professional babies, from a modelling agency. All bonny three- or four-month-olds. Old enough to smile, which is all they were required to do, on the very last frame. I was the only one there working for free. (I had momentarily dallied with the thought of charging a fee to the Department of Health, and then donating it to the Diamond Cot Death Appeal. But Mike said I shouldn't push my luck.)

We did about forty-eight takes. The twenty-fourth, and the last one, were the best. Ironically, by the time I'd got to take forty-eight, we'd come around to using the first baby again. It was a hard day. Terence Donovan wanted the whole message done in one single shot, with me walking into frame, approaching a cot, and lying the baby down on his back. It sounds simple enough, but it's murder when you've got to speak lines at the same time, walk in exactly the right spots, put the baby down at precisely the right moment, and get it to smile perfectly on cue.

Like the colour scheme for the Back to Sleep logo, everything was grey and white. My skin tones and the baby's were the only hint of colour. It's not how I would have done it – I'd have used warmth and colour. But then, I'm not Terence Donovan. He's the millionaire.

I wore a simple cream silk Marks & Spencers blouse, but I

was still rather chubby after my pregnancy. With all that had happened, I hadn't given my health or fitness a moment's thought. So the dress designer got a pair of scissors, and slit the blouse right up the back, so that it fell loosely and easily around the front. No-one would see.

At the end of the shoot, I wandered back to the make-up and wardrobe area. I glanced back at the mêlée of activity. Cameraman and producers, sound recordists and engineers, babies and their mothers, scriptwriters from the Health Education Authority. *'Oh, Supi, if only you were here to see all this,'* I whispered. *'This is probably the most important thing I'll ever do in my whole life and it's all because of you…'*

The Health Minister and I became, in her words 'a marvellous double act' on the morning that we launched the Back to Sleep campaign. I think, however, that she used the term sarcastically rather than out of any genuine pride. It seemed that wherever she turned up to be interviewed that morning, I was in her wake. By the look of astonishment on her face, I could tell that she had not been warned she would be sharing the spotlight.

We first met at TV-am at seven o'clock, where we sat on the breakfast couch together to be interviewed by Mike Morris and Lorraine Kelly. We presented the all-important united front, and I sat and smiled as the Health Minister proudly announced her life-saving initiative. To have bickered at this point about whose idea it had actually been, or to have reminded her that she had needed more than a little persuasion, would have diluted the message.

This was the moment that I, too, played politician.

The journalists weren't fooled – and many of them tried to get me to criticize the government. But today, I said, was not the day for such argument. Today we had news that every parent at home would want to hear. Political rowing would simply turn them off.

We continued on our cot death roadshow, in separate cars –

Mrs B. with her minder and me with my bacon sandwich – to Sky News and BBC Radio. Finally, we were interviewed in separate locations by *BBC Breakfast Time*. And then we stood together for photographs at the press conference, where the ad was played to reporters, and the campaign leaflets were on show.

I looked around the room. Everyone who was anyone in the cot death world was there. They had pulled together the Royal College of Midwives, the Foundation for the Study of Infant Deaths, Peter Fleming – even the Chief Executive of Mothercare, Derek Lovelock, who was promising to distribute the government leaflets in his stores. It was magnificent, even if Mike was still muttering about the clumsiness of the 'Ack to Sleep' message. We both giggled when one reporter came up to us and asked us what it meant. He couldn't see it either!

I read the words at the bottom of the poster. It said:

Cot death is comparatively rare.

*Recent research, however, has shown that if babies
are laid down to sleep on their back or side, the
risk of cot death can be greatly reduced.*

*Don't be worried that they might be sick and choke
when on their back. There is no evidence that this happens.*

*However, there are some babies with special medical
problems who need to sleep on their front.*

*And some babies are used to sleeping on their tummy.
Try the new position but if the baby finds it too
distressing, it is probably wiser not to persist.*

*If you have any doubts at all, don't hesitate to
contact your doctor, midwife or health visitor.*

*And remember, once babies are strong enough to
roll over by themselves, they can sleep in any
position they like.*

*The Department of Health's new leaflet explains in
more detail how anyone who looks after a baby can
help reduce the risk of cot death.*

*It's indispensable advice. And if you ask for your
copy today, it won't just keep your baby safer,
it'll help you sleep more easily, too.*

The Freepost address was, quite by coincidence, in Bristol.
I thought that was apt.

It was everything I'd wanted the campaign to be. Getting it
out of the government had been, as they say, like pulling teeth.
I congratulated the Health Minister, and she smiled sweetly. I
had hoped, at this final moment, to see a hint of humanity,
even compassion, in her eyes. She was a mother, too. Couldn't
she see how important all of this was to me?

To give her her due, she was probably thinking of the next
fire. She probably had another three or four deputations of
desperate people waiting outside her office in Richmond
House. She whisked off to her meetings, and her busy, busy
schedule. I went back home – to try and figure out what we'd
all do now the campaigning was over.

Chapter 25

They were right, of course, those cot death experts. They had all warned me that I should be at home grieving the death of my son, instead of blazing a campaign trail. I remember Shirley Tonkin's words: 'You may think you can avoid it, but grief must be lived through – or you won't properly recover. When you get home, it will hit you like a sledgehammer...'

And it did. Maybe it was because the fire and fury of our crusade had now dissipated. The children were back at school – in fact, Oliver had started full time Big School, and the house seemed very empty. Or maybe it was just delayed reaction, but I sank into a deep hole of sadness, particularly at night. I just could not sleep. All night I would re-enact the trials of the previous weeks. I would sit in empty offices in Richmond House, thumping the table at various faceless politicians. Over and over again, I would replay the video tape in my head of the morning I found Supi dead. As Mike Morris had said in his letter, nothing would erase the vision. But I didn't want it erased, I just wanted a different ending.

Why hadn't I done what so many other women had told me in their letters? Why hadn't I followed my own mother's example, and put my baby down to sleep on his back, or side? Why hadn't we gone for our usual Christmas holiday in Australia? The Australian cot death campaign would have been in full swing that Christmas before Supi's birth, following the example of the New Zealanders. I would have seen it. I would have followed their advice. Supi would be alive.

And when I did fall asleep, I would have that dream, again

and again. I would run down that long corridor to the man behind the mahogany desk, screaming: 'Now, can I have my baby back?'

In the morning, Mike would look at me over the breakfast cereal. 'You look terrible!'

'Yes,' I would sigh. 'I've been campaigning all night...'

We decided to escape. We wanted to go as far away as possible. Now that I'd made the cot death advert, the last thing I wanted was to see it every time I turned on the TV. We rented a house in Palm Beach, just up the coast from Sydney in Australia, and took the whole family, including Mike's parents.

I'd long ago learned the best way to amuse little boys on a long, twenty-four-hour flight. Wads of paper, boxes of washable fluorescent felt tip pens and rolls of Sellotape. For what seemed like days on end, Mike's mum and I sat cutting out, drawing and sticking with Oliver and Jamie, putting our imaginations and creativity to their utmost challenge. We made glove puppets, Ninja Turtle masks, Christmas bunting and story books – and special carrier bags to stick on the back of the seat in front. It kept us going until Bangkok, when sleep overcame everyone – and we stayed comatose until the little plane on the computer graphic displayed above our heads entered Australasian airspace.

Sydney was where Jamie was born. We had come back to give him a birthday party on the beach. But you cannot escape grief. It follows you across the world. And even though we thought that a Christmas under a searing sun might not seem so emotionally charged as in Britain, it was.

We were shopping one afternoon, at Darling Harbour, where the Sydney-siders had developed their old harbour frontage into a spanking new shops and leisure complex. A procession was passing by, along the pedestrianized cobble-stone street. There were children, dressed in biblical clothes, leading baby lambs, goats and piglets. The children were mesmerized. It was a pageant – and when three camels appeared, with some very regal-looking kings astride them – it became obvious that a nativity scene was about to be re-enacted.

We joined in the procession, which led to a vast grassy auditorium in the shadow of Sydney's famous Harbour Bridge. Programmes, songbooks, and candles were for sale. We sat on the grass, Mike, his parents, Toni and Bertie, Oliver, Jamie and I, and watched a magical, musical extravaganza of the nativity story, as the sun set in the sky beyond, and a huge moon rose above the Sydney Tower.

Australian children sing 'Silent Night', too. You can't get away from it. Not even if you run 12,000 miles from home. We sang along, holding our candles up to the dark sky, and wept for the little boy who should have been with us.

Back home, I went to see one of the doctors at our local GP surgery, Roy McGregor, another TV doctor whose practice happened to be near us. I knew Roy, mostly from having interviewed him on TV-am. Now I took one look at him, and started to blub.

'Please give me something to help me go to sleep,' I appealed to him. I was desperate for valium – anything that would knock me out.

To his eternal credit, he refused. He sat me down, and made me talk about the problem. 'What you want is a bit of counselling,' he said. 'It will make you feel a lot better than sleeping pills.'

I couldn't see how. Nothing was going to make me feel better, since the pain was being caused by Supi's death. And I realized now that nothing was going to bring him back.

'Give it a try, just give it a try,' he pleaded. 'If it doesn't help, then give it up and come back to see me. But promise me you'll see a counsellor first.'

He gave me the name of a bereavement counsellor he knew and trusted. She was called Vivienne and she lived five minutes from my front door. I rang her, and found that she was expecting my call. When I walked into the little room which she had set aside in her house for her work, I noticed straight away the box of tissues on the table. The tools of her trade? I wasn't the sort of person who ever cried in public. I always managed somehow, even on the most tense of occasions, to hold back until I was alone. But two minutes into our conversation, and I was pulling tissue after tissue out of the box, and blowing my nose like an emotional wreck. I was embarrassed to be so raw in front of a total stranger, but I just couldn't help it.

I don't know what we talked about, except that I loved Supi and wanted him back. But that night, I slept. So I went back to see Vivienne again, and my nights of sleep grew longer and more frequent. We talked about big things – like religious belief, and whether I believed that Supi had gone to Heaven. We talked about tiny things – minuscule worries that might have seemed insignificant to anyone else, but were beginning to haunt me. Like what should we do with his bedroom? Where should I put his clothes? Should I keep his mattress? Was it healthy for me still to sleep with his baby sleepsuit under my pillow? She taught me that nearly any feeling was OK, providing it didn't become obsessive.

At one point, when Mike and I were considering moving house, I told her that I was worried I might be leaving him behind in some way. Years before, I had seen a TV play called *The Stone Tapes*. It had explored the theory that spiritual energy could be absorbed by the very walls around us. I was still wrestling with the mystery of what had happened to Supi's spirit, the spark of life that had so clearly left his body that dreadful morning. I wasn't particularly religious, but I kept asking myself 'What if?' I didn't want to leave that room behind, his wallpaper, his walls.

'Well, if you are that worried, then take them with you...' Vivienne said.

'How?' I asked.

'Nothing is impossible,' she said. 'If you want to take that wallpaper with you, then steam it off the walls. Take the plaster, too, if you really want to.'

I laughed, nervously.

'I mean it,' she said. 'If you really want to do it, then you can. Think about it.'

And, of course, from that moment onwards, there was really no need. I stopped worrying about it. And when the day came to leave our London house behind, I had passed beyond my *Stone Tapes* theory, and on to something else. The point is, Vivienne had given me *permission* to feel the strangest and weirdest of feelings. She hadn't laughed, nor dismissed them – she had actually validated them. And while she couldn't bring Supi back, I was somehow feeling a little better.

On one of our last afternoons in that London garden, I was pottering in the flower beds while Oliver and Jamie played on the grass. I had become a keen gardener since Supi died, though very much a beginner. It somehow helped me to plant things, nurture them and watch them grow. Maybe I still needed visual confirmation that I could raise something living and keep it alive. They were chuckling loudly, and I turned around quickly to see what had amused them so much. I could swear I saw a little boy playing with them. I knew it was Supi. And I smiled. It was the first time, since we had lost him, that I had thought of Supi without the first sensation being one of pain. Now I knew I could remember him with feelings of joy as well. It felt like a release.

Chapter 26

'Do you think you'll ever have another baby?' It was a disarmingly direct question, but coming as it did from another bereaved parent, it didn't seem like a heartless intrusion. We were in Dublin, in the Green Room of RTE, the Irish television station – and we'd just appeared on the *Kenny Live* show, one of the highest rated chat shows in Ireland.

Mike and I were in Ireland as the guests of ISIDA, the Irish Sudden Infant Death Association. They were negotiating with the Irish government to launch a similar campaign to ours. When they'd rung us, they'd been so sincere and committed, that we had wanted to rush to help them. When we got there, we found out why we were so drawn. All of the members were bereaved parents – none of them were professional charity workers. It seemed to make a difference. To us, at least.

Hardly were we on Irish soil, than out of the small delegation which met us, one couple stepped forward and hugged us eagerly. 'Anne, Mike, welcome! We're Una and Brian O'Brien.' I knew them straight away. They had sat down and written to us on the day Supi died, as soon as they heard the news. They were the couple from Ireland who had lost their baby daughter Sorcha, on July the twelfth exactly one year before. It's difficult to describe the immediate closeness you feel at a moment like that. When those two people had written, telling us their sad story and sympathizing with ours, they had formed a special bond. Every 12 July, while we are wrestling with the now twin emotions of happiness at Oliver's birthday, and sadness at Supi's anniversary, we think of Una and Brian too.

Now we were in Ireland, campaigning for Irish babies. We had spoken to their press, appeared on their chat show, and spoken to a meeting of experts and parents. They'd invited Peter Fleming, too. And for the first time, we saw him deliver a lecture. It was the lecture about the discovery in Avon of the breakthrough concerning sleeping position.

'If this doesn't convince our government, I don't know what will!' said an Irish father present. And then he asked it again, softly. 'Do you think you'll ever have another baby, then?'

If anyone else had asked, I think I would have been offended. I would have taken it as an insult to Supi. But this man, and all the other people around us, knew what it was like to lose a child. They had written their own code of 'What To Do and Say' in a leaflet for the family and friends of newly bereaved parents. And number one on that list was *Don't tell them they've got a little angel in Heaven, because they don't want to hear it.* That made me warm to them straightaway. It had been said to us so often. They were right – you really don't want to hear about little angels in Heaven. You want your baby here on earth.

These people had been through it. And they also understood the mixed emotions you felt when considering having more children. They had felt the guilt, the worry and the feelings of betrayal. They *knew.* They had been there. I could talk to them. We were in the same boat.

Everyone watched for my response, including Mike. 'Oh! I don't know!' I laughed. 'Sometimes I think it would be nice, and the rest of the time I'm not so sure...'

'Ah, well, then,' smiled the Irishman, a twinkle in his eye. 'Tis an accident you'll be wanting...'

But the accident was a long time coming. By the end of our second year without Supi, I was longing for another baby. By now, I knew that it wouldn't be Supi. And I was also sure that it wouldn't be a replacement. I just needed a live, kicking baby in my arms. It's like that friend of mine had said: 'You're still the mother of a four-month-old baby, even though the baby has gone.' It's not that Oliver and Jamie did not fulfil my maternal instincts. I loved them as much as I'd ever done. Maybe only another mother understands. I needed a baby. And that baby was Jake.

When I discovered I was pregnant, I was so excited I could barely contain the news. Mike was at work, and I had to wait several hours before I could sit him down and tell him. We had recently started working at the BBC in Birmingham, making a coffee-time programme called *Good Morning with Anne and Nick*. The BBC had come to Mike, and asked him to revamp their morning output. Eventually, it had come down to the creation of one programme – a magazine of topical features, fashion, chat and medical news.

It meant that Nick Owen and I could be reunited – something we'd wanted ever since he'd left TV-am – and we could present a show edited by Mike, in whom we both had utmost confidence. Where the BBC had a pretty shoddy reputation for its morning output, we knew Mike would be able to shield us from the notorious 'dead hand' of the BBC – and produce a show sufficiently bright and brilliant to beat *This Morning* on the other channel.

Ironically, the man from the BBC who came to our London house to persuade us to up sticks and go to Birmingham, was a cot death father, too. His name was David Waine. He and his wife Liz, had lost their baby daughter many years before.

Mike came home that evening in a flurry of paperwork, BBC memos, and videos, with his mobile phone forever ringing. I couldn't get a quiet moment with him until the children were in bed, and we were getting ready to sleep ourselves.

'Mike, I think I'm pregnant...' In fact, I *knew* I was. But I was going to break this news gently, in case he had a shock.

Instead, his eyes brimmed with tears. 'Do you think we can go through this again?' I asked him.

He looked at me and smiled. 'Of course we can,' he whispered, and then cried.

Nine months later Jake was born, the spitting image of his brothers. Maggie Thom delivered him, and the team of midwives who looked after him in his first few days were the same team which had cared for Supi. I sat up in my bed, cuddling my new little baby with the tuft of dark hair which had led his Dad to call him 'Spike', and counted my blessings.

Four. And as I was rocking my fourth, I heard Julia Somerville, the newsreader, on *News at Ten*. 'And finally... we've just heard that television presenter and cot death campaigner Anne Diamond has given birth to a baby boy. It is two years since the cot death of her third son, Sebastian. Mother and baby are said to be doing well.' And then Julia added her own congratulations, and said goodnight. I looked down at the little bundle and noticed that, for the first time in ages, my arms were not aching. They were full...of wriggling baby.

On the day Jake and I were due to leave hospital, Mike came in with Nanny Alex and the two big boys.

'We stopped off at the church and lit a candle for Supi,' said Alex. 'The boys told God that they loved their new baby. And do you know what they said then?'

'No, what?' I asked Oliver and Jamie.

Oliver took up the story. 'I asked God if we could keep this one,' he said. 'We can, can't we Mummy?'

Dr Rom came in to give Jake his final check-up. Just as he had done before with Supi, he gently undressed him, and went through his various bits and pieces. Hips OK, upper palette, lower palette, ten fingers (including two thumbs), ten toes. Everything complete and in full working order.

'This is a wonderful day,' he said quietly, but to the whole room. 'Little Jake is a new life – and we welcome him into the world. But we will never forget Sebastian. I never will. Whenever I give the sleeping position advice to my new mums, I am proud to tell them that Sebastian was one of my babies. Now you go off and take this little chap home. And, of course, when he goes to sleep, he will sleep on his...' At this, he turned to the boys, quizzically.

'Back!' they chorused.

Epilogue

I cannot say Jake's first few months were easy, because they were not. He caught a cold, and for many nights I lay awake just listening to him breathe.

We were enrolled, before he was born, on the CONI (Care of the Next Infant) scheme, a programme set up initially by the Foundation for the Study of Infant Death. This meant that we were put under the care of a local paediatrician specially trained in the care of families who go on to have another baby after a cot death. On the scheme, you can, if you want, borrow a breathing monitor. At first I had rejected one, having experienced monitors before. But I couldn't stay awake all night every night watching Jake's chest go up and down, so finally I succumbed.

I was lent a Densa monitor, the sort you fix around the baby's chest with elastic, just like the one I had seen in New Zealand. It was easy to use, and gave me great peace of mind. We hardly ever had a false alarm. We were also lent special baby scales, and kept a graph of his weight gain, so that the health visitor, nanny and I could easily spot any sign of trouble in his health.

I did something too, that I had never done with my first three children. I had Jake in bed with me all through the night. I don't know why I had never considered it before. Probably because I had been so proud to decorate and equip a brand new nursery for each of them. Maybe because I had always had a nanny to help. But it had never actually occurred to me, after the first few days, to keep them in my bed, nor even in my bedroom unless they were ill. It was a wonderful experience. Every night I would go to sleep happily, hearing him breathe almost in my ear. And in the mornings, he would turn to see me, and beam.

Mike, though, was not so thrilled. Naturally he had the same worries as me about our new baby surviving the night – but he's the sort of sleeper who cannot bear to be disturbed. Once he has woken up, he cannot get back to sleep. Many was the night I found him sitting up in bed watching satellite TV, watching over a sleeping Jake. I, meanwhile, had fed and changed the baby, trudged along the corridor to check the big boys, and happily dozed off again.

When Jake got so big that he kicked us in the ribs for space, we bought a marvellous invention called a Bedside Bed. It's basically a cot with three sides, designed to butt up against your own bed, and with adjustable height so that the baby's cot effectively becomes an extension to your own bed. I was still worried about the dangers of possibly rolling over on to Jake, or of him overheating underneath our duvet. This Bedside Bed, I thought, was the perfect solution. He was next to me, always within my arm's reach, and yet he was lying safely in his own environment, with his own bedclothes.

One morning I was contacted by Joyce Epstein, from the Foundation. She said they were arranging a press conference to announce new guidelines for mothers about co-sleeping. Would I come along and help? They had decided to actively campaign against the practice of mothers sleeping with their babies in the same bed. I squirmed with embarrassment. How could I advise mothers to do something which I was doing myself and enjoying? Was it really wrong to sleep with your child? I made some feeble excuse, and declined the invitation.

One night, when Jake was about eleven months old, I awoke in terror. The alarm on his breathing monitor was beeping loudly, and the red light flashing. I leaned over to him. His face looked shocked, and then he started to cry. I switched the light on, and looked him over. Once he had calmed down, he

236

seemed fine. My heart was still leaping out of my chest. But nothing seemed to be wrong. Maybe he had simply held his breath a little too long. The monitor was programmed to go off if there was no breath for twenty seconds. I fixed it around his chest again, and we both settled down to sleep.

An hour later, the same thing happened. And an hour after that. And again. That night, Jake set the alarm off five times. I was shattered, and very worried. Was Jake, even at this mature age, showing a breathing problem? Could he have died those five times, if the alarm hadn't warned me? Or was the alarm going bananas?

I phoned our CONI paediatrician, Eve Fleming (no relation to Peter). I went into work as usual, to present my programme, leaving Nanny Alex with strict instructions to watch Jake like a hawk, and attach the monitor to him for his morning nap. Then, after the programme had ended, I rushed home, meeting Alex with Jake, and the monitor, at the paediatrician's surgery.

She checked him over. There was nothing wrong. In fact, he was the picture of health. Quite a bruiser.

'If you want, we could admit him to hospital for observation...but he seems to be quite well. It might be the monitor itself. We'll send it away to get it checked. Meanwhile, use a brand new one...'

So we tried again. But that night, the very same thing happened. In fact, the alarm sounded six or seven times. On the third night, I stayed awake all night, and watched what happened. Sure enough, the alarm sounded. But Jake had been breathing normally, or so it seemed.

I rang Peter Fleming, in Bristol. He could hear my tension down the phone. 'Do you want him to come in for observation?' he asked.

'I don't think so. Not yet, anyway. But I wish I knew why he's setting the alarm off so much...' Cot death was still possible. Even at eleven months.

'Well, if you can come here, I'll lend you a piece of hospital equipment called an oximeter. That will at least tell you if his oxygen levels are safe.'

So I drove that afternoon to Bristol, and received a crash instruction course on attaching such a monitor to a stroppy eleven-month-old baby. Basically, I waited until Jake was asleep, and then I taped a special device around his big toe. A red light shone through his flesh, and measured the oxygen levels in his blood. I had seen one before, on Supi when he had been in special care.

Meanwhile, Jake was also attached to his usual monitor. There were so many machines blipping and beeping that our bedroom looked like a hospital's intensive care unit. I stayed up all night again, staring at Jake, who slept on knowing nothing of the anxiety he was causing. At about two in the morning, the alarm sounded. My eyes shot to Jake. He was breathing normally. I looked at the oximeter. It was reading healthy levels of oxygen. *I* breathed again. It happened four more times that night. I left for work the next morning, troubled but happier at least that Jake seemed to be breathing well, despite the alarms.

'It sounds to me as though he's just too old to be using the monitor,' suggested Mark Porter, our TV doctor. 'Maybe it's time to think of giving it up. I know it's hard, but you're going to have to, at some point!'

And that's exactly what Peter Fleming reckoned, too. 'What we say at times like this,' he said, and I could hear the smile, 'is that the interface between baby and monitor is no longer working efficiently...'

So Mike and I summed up all our courage, and took Jake off his monitor. I think he was happy to see it go. We never looked back. There were often moments, particularly at night when Jake and I would cuddle before he dropped off to sleep, that I would tell him about the brother he'd never know. But he'd look at me with such mischievous eyes that I'd wonder. Did he know Supi? Had they, perhaps, bumped into each other in that place called Heaven, when they were souls all busy working out their karma? Or am I still kidding myself with fanciful notions, in the endless quest for peace of mind?

One thing's for sure – Jake has been an absolute miracle. He was never for one moment another child's replacement. From his first cry, he established his own strong personality. He filled my arms, and our lives with his boisterous demands. He has helped us overcome whatever emotional hurdles still stood in our path to recovery, and I'll always be grateful to him for that. Had Supi lived, we would probably not have gone on to have yet another child, our little Jacob. So we look upon him as a gift – not just from God, but also from Sebastian.

Now we have another gift, too, or more a surprise bonus – our little Conor, born on St Patrick's Day, 1995. Another little miracle, who looks at the moment exactly like his missing brother. But no doubt he'll develop in his own way – and will one day be his own man. We are blessed.

A while ago Oliver came up to me and patted my stomach. 'Exactly how many babies have you got in there?' he asked, as if he felt overloaded with the responsibility of being Big Brother to such a large team. I think that's it, Ollie. I'll tell you all about it when you're older.

Six months after the Back to Sleep campaign was launched, the cot death rate in Britain had halved. That means, in simplistic layman's terms, that about 500 babies *didn't* die who otherwise would have. Just in the first six months. A year later, the cot death rate had fallen by an overall sixty-nine per cent. And it continues to fall. More and more babies live to see the morning.

Once the message was relayed throughout Britain, it must have saved lives literally *overnight*. And when the Department of Health conducted a survey to find out how people had gleaned the new advice, they found that eighty-seven per cent of people had got it from the television ad. That made me feel better about thumping Mrs B.'s table.

I watched her, a year later, on the TV, talking about the need for a campaign to promote the measles vaccination. She said it would have to be as good as the cot death campaign. 'The Back to Sleep campaign is the most successful public health campaign we've ever had,' she said proudly.

Of course, that makes me feel good. But what of those wasted lives? My Sebastian isn't the only baby who need not have died. Four other babies died on the same day as Supi. Another four the next day, and the next , and the next – 2,000 that very year. And all that time, we could have been actively campaigning to save nearly two thirds of them. We were culpably slow to act.

Throughout this country there are mothers and fathers whose hearts are breaking for their lost children. I know. I've got letters from most of them. One of them's a lawyer, in Mortlake, London. She tells me we should sue the Government for negligence. Another is a GP, who feels so disillusioned with her own profession that she can hardly bear to go back to work. At times I am strong enough to be philosophical, and shrug my shoulders and tell myself not to look back with revenge or bitterness. At other times I miss Sebastian so much I want to throttle any sign of the complacency which allowed him to die. I'd love to sue somebody, if I thought it would do any good.

It's generally thought that the trend for lying babies on their stomachs came from the United States of America. That's where doctors first started to save tiny neo-nates, babies born well before their due dates, and where Special Care Baby Units were developed. They discovered that premature babies fared much better on their stomachs, and so the prone sleeping position quickly became a vital part of neo-natal care. Indeed, the popular image of the happy, well-tended baby became that of a baby lying on its tummy, sucking its thumb. I'm sure you've seen it.

240

Somehow, somewhere, *someone* then thought that the same principle should apply to ordinary, term, healthy babies, too. And that, it appears, is where they went wrong. Of course, the prone position is safe for the *vast majority* of babies. Oliver and Jamie slept on their tummies and lived. But for some babies, it is terribly dangerous, it makes them susceptible to cot death. The trouble is, no-one can tell you *which ones*.

Now, the world is turning upside down. Throughout Europe, in Canada, and even in America, governments are launching cot death campaigns. We nearly lost Dr Peter Fleming to the Canadians, in their enthusiasm to save lives. He had been helping them prepare their campaign, inspiringly called 'Sweet Dreams', when they sneakily offered him the chair of paediatric medicine at Toronto University. The Foundation, who had already funded an enormous project for him, asked the Diamond Cot Death Appeal to help. With an extra £100,000 from our fund, together we kept him in Britain.

Speak to any mum or dad in any hospital in any part of the world, and they'll tell you that they idolize the doctor who saved their baby's life. Well, Peter Fleming didn't save mine, but I think he *would have*, had we known him. One thing's for certain, he has saved countless hundreds – no, thousands – of lives. But he has never received so much as a thank you letter. Because those mums and dads who've been spared the tragedy of cot death don't even know it. I would like to say thanks, on their behalf, Peter. And to Shirley Tonkin, and Ed Mitchell, and all the other brave, stubborn and talented people in this country and elsewhere who cared enough to find out why our babies died – and, more importantly, what could be done about it.

There's a tiny little room in St Michael's Hospital in Bristol, with a large double bed and lots of wires linked up to monitors and an infra-red camera. Inside the bed, tucked up warmly under the duvet, is a young mother with her new baby. They're both fast asleep, subconsciously revelling in the almost primitive closeness of those first special days – and nights – together. But they're being watched, on a close circuit TV screen. Their heart rates, oxygen saturation, body temperatures, brain waves – and all sorts of bodily functions – are being carefully monitored, recorded and analysed. They are the latest recruits to the 'Sebastian Diamond Mother and Baby Sleep Laboratory'. A grand name for such a little room, designed to study the interactions between mothers and babies when they're sleeping together. It's part of the ongoing search for the answer to cot death.

When I first saw the sign on the door, I had to grab Peter's arm to steady myself. I had never seen Supi's name on anything before, even though he's old enough now for me to be sewing nametapes into his school uniform. I'm very proud of you, Supi, I thought. And then I looked at the next door, to the neighbouring laboratory. It said FSID – paid for and sponsored by the Foundation.

I thought of all the other little babies represented by those four initials. Babies every bit as wonderful and important to their parents as Sebastian is to us. Babies whose names did not make headlines, even though – added together – their deaths would have constituted one of the worst human disasters the world has known. Babies whose parents have been where we've been, and would do almost anything to prevent it happening to anyone else. Thousands of babies.

I asked my big boys the other day if they really could remember Supi.

'Oh yes,' replied Oliver. 'We used to play eyebrows with him...'

It was something I'd forgotten. Oh, God. It was something about him that I had forgotten. How could I possibly forget anything about him? And yet I had. He had used to sit in his bouncy chair, in the middle of the playroom, and beckon his brothers over – or so they thought – by raising his eyebrows and looking quizzical. Then they would wiggle their eyebrows

242

at him, and it would always make him gurgle and chuckle.

'Mummy,' asked Jamie, 'is Supi still a baby, or is he getting older all the time, like us?'

I told Jamie the absolute truth. 'I don't know, I'm afraid. No-one knows.' And I turned the question around: 'What do you think?'

'I think he's a baby, because then he can play with baby Jesus.'

'Well, that's rubbish,' snorted Oliver. 'Because baby Jesus isn't a baby. He's a man, because the Romans crucified him...'

Nowadays we often have such deep, philosophical discussions. Like why Supi didn't leave a fossilized skeleton, as the dinosaurs did. That one required a very lengthy and difficult – but always truthful – explanation!

We returned to Cyprus for another holiday – but everything had changed. John and Roswitha had moved away, after having a terrible car accident, and Oliver and Jamie were bored without instant access to a theme park. I unpacked my holiday clothes – the sort that only ever get worn abroad. And there, in the pocket of my sundress, was a baby's sock. It was Supi's.

I held it to my face, and breathed it in. It smelt of him. I buried my face in it, and breathed through it and cried, and wrung it in my hands. Until the sweet smell of little baby had gone for ever.

Conclusion

To answer Oliver's question (did we find the answer to cot death?), I think I can safely say yes, we did. A great deal of the answer anyway.

Cot death is, as the experts have long said, 'multi-factorial', by which they mean that it probably has many causes, some of which are now known, and some of which are not. I think that it is a matter of balance. While our babies may look robust, their lives are being affected every day and every night by many different factors, working both for and against them. Most babies, most of the time, have the weights happily stacked in their favour. But for babies like Sebastian, unseen dangers of which we are only just becoming aware, are massing against them. One too many and the balance tips.

Sebastian was a baby boy, the weaker sex physiologically. He was also premature with breathing problems. He had tiny little health difficulties, like the hydrocele and the oral thrush – unimportant in isolation – yet did they betray a slight fragility? He was four months old, known to be an age when all sorts of physiological changes are going on. It was a hot night, he was in a room on his own, he was lying on a sheepskin and he was in the prone sleeping position. I know now that we had chicken-pox in the house. Could that infection have caused, as it did in my older children, a sudden rise in body temperature? Cancel out just one of those factors, and he may well have survived the night.

If cot death is, as is becoming evident, something to do with a baby's inability to regulate his own temperature, causing or coupled with respiratory failure, then you can see how sleeping

244

position is so important. If a baby is face down, he covers a huge part of the surface area he would normally use to dissipate body heat. Whatever was working against Supi that night, I strongly believe that turning him over would have given him that extra chance. It would probably have tipped the scales back in his favour.

Knowing that, and seeing what I've seen at the Sebastian Diamond Sleep Laboratory in Bristol, I would never leave a baby of that age on his own all night either. Despite all the problems that sleeping with your baby can bring – like your husband moving out of the room, your other children being jealous or your baby being difficult to wean out of your bedroom – I think you'd be stunned if you'd witnessed what I did.

In the Sleep Laboratory, Dr Fleming and his team watch the interaction between a mother and her baby as they sleep. On the first night, the mums and babies sleep as they normally do at home, either with the baby in the bed, or a in a cot next to the bed. For the second night, they do the opposite. On their third visit, they go back to their normal practice.

It was a first visit for this particular mum and baby – and they slept as they did at home, with the mother lying on her side, almost on her tummy, and her child nestling under the crook of her arm. Their faces were only a matter of three or four inches apart. At first when I saw their sleeping images, I worried that they were almost too close. One false move I thought, and the mother will be leaning on her baby. But that just didn't happen. What happened instead was a revelation to me, and a confirmation that nature really does know best.

There were many, many times in the night when mother and baby stirred – sometimes apparently in isolation from each other, at other times cutely in syncopation. It was rather like a dance. At one point, in the midst of a period of deep sleep for both of them, the baby started to fidget slightly, and in a sound almost below normal hearing levels, squeaked like a little mouse, though still fast asleep. The mother subconsciously caressed her child's head, rearranged the bedclothes around them both, patted and stroked the baby, and then settled back into stillness. She had never even half-woken. It was a fleeting moment of sweet tenderness, but it was also much more. Because when we looked at the monitor displays which we could superimpose on to the video, we could see that those few actions had all meant something.

When the baby squeaked and fidgeted, the read-out showed that his surface temperature was becoming warmer than his core temperature. Effectively that meant that the baby was becoming too hot. When the mother heard his noise, she acted. And even though she was asleep, she immediately sensed what her baby needed, adjusted the bedding and the baby's temperature instantly returned to a steady normal level. When asked about it the next morning, the mother was not aware that the incident, or any other periods of interaction, had happened at all. It was totally instinctive.

So what! I can hear the cry of co-sleepers up and down the land. Do I really need a sleep laboratory to tell me that it's natural for mothers and babies to sleep together? Well, no. I suppose I don't. But we now live in a society where it isn't always possible, or indeed desirable, to sleep with our babies. And we need to understand what it is we are *missing out on*, if we decide not to. It may be more than an aesthetic pleasure, it may be vitally important.

One thing we do know, is that you shouldn't sleep with your baby in the same bed as you if you or your partner have been smoking or drinking alcohol. An intoxicated mother can lose the instinct which stops us rolling over on to our babies. A parent who has smoked can go on breathing out toxic fumes in his or her breath for up to four hours after the last cigarette. And passive smoking is highly dangerous for babies. After sleeping position, smoking is the biggest single cause of cot death. All studies throughout the world agree that if experts could stop parents smoking, the cot death rate would plummet.

As for breastfeeding, the New Zealanders were adamant that their study showed it helped to prevent cot death, and so they included it in their risk reduction campaign. The British are equally adamant that although breastfeeding is best for babies in lots of other ways, it makes no difference when it comes to cot death. You can imagine my relief when I heard that one!

There's no doubt for me though, that babies who sleep on their backs sleep much more lightly and for shorter periods than babies who sleep on their tummies. Both Jake and Conor as tiny babies spent most of the night stirring, squeaking and squirming, and regularly kicking the bedclothes off. Many times during the night I would muse upon the natural way they were regulating their temperature, as I replaced the sheet over their legs, only to repeat the process an hour or two later.

Mattresses? Years ago, when it was alleged that babies may have inhaled toxic fumes from the fire-retardant chemicals on some cot mattresses, the government should have investigated the theory. In fact, they had failed to clear the matter up completely. Now, after yet more pressure from TV documentaries like *The Cook Report* on ITV, they have agreed on a full enquiry. Initial reports indicate that there is unlikely to be a link between cot mattresses and cot death. I have covered my mattress with a 'protective cot sheet', designed to protect a mattress from bedwetting, just in case. The scientists tell us that these sheets contain no harmful chemicals themselves, and would be an effective barrier against any chemicals in the mattress.

I am inundated with letters from worried mothers asking about various gadgets and wedges, designed to stop your baby from rolling over on to his tummy. Dr Fleming says that anything which falsely inhibits your baby's natural movements – and might therefore distress him – cannot be doing him any good. And anyway, they could contribute to overheating.

As for monitors, the popular line from the experts is that

'breathing monitors have never been known to save lives'. I think that's a medical cop-out. They simply don't know, and they are scared that every parent in the land will demand a highly expensive monitor. I use one because my baby died, but I also know what hell they are if you don't have full back-up from your GP, Health Visitor and paediatrician (all with cot death training) and thorough instruction in how to use and understand them. I'm tempted to say that with the risk reduction rules we already know, we do not need monitors, but I haven't the courage to give mine back. I do believe, however, that every parent in the land should be given full instruction on how to give a baby the kiss of life. When you think of it, it's criminal that we aren't all taught it at school.

We are still losing babies to cot death. Every week, ten families go through the hell we still endure. I get letters from women who scream at me from the page: 'Anne, we did everything you said, and we still lost our baby!' It's a curious fact that even before the Back to Sleep campaign, whenever there was a scare about cot death, the death toll went down fractionally. Indeed, some sceptics said at first that the Back to Sleep campaign was nothing more than the same reaction on a larger scale. That would suggest that parents suddenly take better care of their children after a scare, which in turn implies that parents are not usually taking *enough* care. That insults most of us.

What is clearly true, is that when there is heightened awareness of cot death and we are more conscious of the vulnerability of our little ones, we feel justified in feeling protective, even paranoid about our children's health and well-being. GPs always report a sudden influx of worried mothers with snuffly, grizzly babies. That may be a good thing. That's why 'going to your GP if you are worried' was included in the Golden Rules of the Back to Sleep campaign. That campaign should be repeated annually – it's absolutely guaranteed that it would result in a further drop in cot death.

Just in case anyone needed further proof, then they should look again at Avon. At the height of the national campaign, and after much campaigning on a local level too, they enjoyed a fifteen-month period where they had *no cot deaths at all. Not a single one. Since then, they have never lost a child to a non-smoking family. These are the facts – they are not opinions.*

Of course, cot deaths in non-smoking households are still happening, but it is rare nowadays for the death to be totally unexplained by known risk factors. Usually, it is possible to see now what elements may have heaped up against the baby and how that vital balance might have been tipped. Sometimes, it is clear that the child had breathing problems, had been premature, had rolled over on to its front, had caught a sudden infection or had suffered a number of problems together. We now know that heightened awareness improves the chances of vulnerable children – simply by giving the parents the right to worry.

I get very fed up with people who say that by talking about cot death, I could ruin a parent's enjoyment of their babies and make them frightened. Mums and Dads are frightened of cot death anyway. They are thirsty for information about it. Now, for the first time ever in the painful history of Sudden Infant Death Syndrome, there is something we ordinary parents can do about it. We can defeat the killer, and enjoy our babies all the more.

Useful Addresses

Cot Death Society (and
Support for Bereaved
Parents)
117 High Street
Worle
Weston-super-Mare
Avon
BS22 0HB
Helpline: 01836 219010

Diamond Cot Death Appeal
Registered Charity No:
801394
Midland Bank Account No:
01122940
Sortcode: 40-07-25
*(You can give money at any
branch with these details)*

Foundation for the Study of
Infant Deaths (FSID)
14 Halkin Street
London
SW1X 7DP
**Cot death 24-hour
manned helpline:
0171 235 1721**
Tel: 0171 235 0965
Fax: 0171 823 1986

Irish Sudden Infant Death
Association (ISIDA)
Carmichael House
4 North Brunswick Street
Dublin 7
**Freephone helpline, open
9am-5pm: (01) 874 7007**
Tel: (01) 873 2711/872 6199
Fax: (01) 872 6056

'Protective Cot Sheet'
Available from branches of
Boots and Mothercare

Scottish Cot Death Trust
Royal Hospital for Sick
Children
Yorkhill
Glasgow
G3 8SJ
Tel: 0141 357 3946
(9am-5pm)
Fax: 0141 334 1376

Sebastian Diamond Sleep
Laboratory
Department of Child Health
St Michael's Hospital
Bristol

Stillbirth and Neonatal
Death Society (SANDS)
28 Portland Place
London
W1N 4DE
Helpline: 0171 436 5881
General enquiries:
0171 436 7940

The Bedside Bed Co.
398 Woodlands Avenue
London
E11 3QY
Tel: 0181 989 8683

The Child Bereavement
Trust
1 Millside
Riversdale
Bourne End
Bucks
OL9 5EB
Tel: 01494 765001
(Mainly for professional carers)

The Compassionate Friends
53 North Street
Bristol
BS3 1EN
Helpline: 0117 953 9639
Tel: 0117 966 5202
*(A nationwide organization of
bereaved parents offering
friendship and understanding
to other bereaved parents. I am
a patron.)*

The Twins and Multiple
Births Association
(TAMBA)
PO Box 30
Little Sutton
South Wirral
L65 1TH
**Twinline (helpline) eves
and weekends:
01732 868000**
General enquiries:
0151 348 0020

Useful Publications

Coping With Cot Death   Sarah Murphy (Sheldon Press, £5.99)

'Reducing The Risk of Cot Death' (leaflet)
Health Publications Unit
No 2 Site
Heywood Stores
Manchester Road
Heywood
Lancs
OL19 2PZ
Tel: 0800 555777
Report of the Chief Medical Officer's Expert Group on 'The Sleeping Position of Infants and Cot Death' (HMSO).
Available through HMSO bookshops and other booksellers.
Tel orders: 0171 873 9090
(This contains all the background information to the Back To Sleep campaign and some of the results and surveys)